UNDER SIX FLAGS

THE STORY OF TEXAS

M. E. M. Davis
AUTHOR OF *In War Times at La Rose Blanche,*
Under the Man-Fig, Minding the Gap, ETC., ETC.

HERITAGE BOOKS
2024

HERITAGE BOOKS
AN IMPRINT OF HERITAGE BOOKS, INC.

Books, CDs, and more—Worldwide

For our listing of thousands of titles see our website
at
www.HeritageBooks.com

A Facsimile Reprint
Published 2024 by
HERITAGE BOOKS, INC.
Publishing Division
5810 Ruatan Street
Berwyn Heights, MD 20740

Copyright © 1897 M. E. M. Davis

— Publisher's Notice —
In reprints such as this, it is often not possible to remove
blemishes from the original. We feel the contents of this
book warrant its reissue despite these blemishes and
hope you will agree and read it with pleasure.

International Standard Book Number
Paperbound: 978-0-7884-8596-1

PREFACE.

In the following pages I have endeavored to sketch, in rather bold outlines, the story of Texas. It is a story of knightly romance which calls the poet even as, in earlier days, the Land of the Tehas called across its borders the dreamers of dreams.

But the history of Texas is far more than a romantic legend. It is a record of bold conceptions and bolder deeds; the story of the discoverer penetrating unknown wildernesses; of the pioneer matching his strength against the savage; of the colonist struggling for his freedom and his rights.

It is the chronicle of the birth of a people; the history of the rise and progress of a great State.

I have tried in these simple readings so to arrange the salient points of a drama of two centuries as to present a consistent whole.

And I shall be happy if I shall succeed in awakening in the reader somewhat of the interest in Texas history which has inspired this work.

There are several features which mark Texas history as unique. One of these is the difference between the methods of colonization employed in Texas and those exercised elsewhere in the United States.

The pioneer with his cabin, his ever-spreading fields, his gardens and orchards — the idea of the home with its roots in the very soil, as represented by Austin and his followers — was preceded by a hundred barren years of fortress and soldier, the Spanish idea of conquest and military rule.

Again, its vast extent of territory and the ease with which its rich lands were acquired seemed to adapt Texas peculiarly to those communistic and utopian experiments which have been the delight of the visionary in every age of the world's progress. A number of these have been tried upon its soil. The result has been to give a varied and original coloring to the shifting scenes.

The philosophical student will find these phases of our history well worth his consideration.

I desire in this place to express my thanks to the Texas teachers, to many of whom I am indebted for timely suggestions and for kindly encouragement; also my grateful obligation to Mr. William Beer, of the New Orleans Howard Memorial Library, for valuable assistance; and to the Library itself, which, under his able direction, has become particularly rich in documents and publications relating to the early history of Louisiana and Texas.

M. E. M. DAVIS.

CONTENTS.

I.

FORT ST. LOUIS.

		PAGE
1.	IN THE NAME OF FRANCE	1
2.	IN THE NAME OF SPAIN	9
3.	IN THE NAME OF OBLIVION	12

II.

SAN ANTONIO.

1.	A BOLD RIDER	14
2.	COWL AND CARBINE	16
3.	A HURRIED RIDE	20
4.	INDIOS BRAVOS	23
5.	ALONG THE OLD SAN ANTONIO ROAD	25

III.

NACOGDOCHES.

1.	A FATAL VENTURE	29
2.	THE DISPUTED BOUNDARY LINE	33
3.	THE NEUTRAL GROUND	36
4.	THE RED HOUSE	40
5.	THE CHAMP D'ASILE	44
6.	A TREACHEROUS SHOT	46
7.	A VOICE IN THE WILDERNESS	48

IV.

SAN FELIPE DE AUSTIN.

1. An Unexpected Meeting 50
2. Ups and Downs 52
3. Orders and Disorders 56
4. A Trumpet Call 62
5. Out of a Mist 65
6. The Priest's House 69
7. By the Brazos 74

V.

GOLIAD.

1. Messengers of Distress 77
2. In Church and Fortress 82
3. Fort Defiance 85
4. Palm Sunday 91
5. Remember the Alamo! Remember Goliad! . . . 96
6. Two Generals 102
7. How the Good News was Brought 105

VI.

HOUSTON.

1. On Buffalo Bayou 111
2. The Invincible 117
3. The Capital 120
4. The War of the Archives 124
5. The Black Beans 127

VII.

AUSTIN.

		PAGE
1.	THE REPUBLIC IS NO MORE	132
2.	ACROSS THE BORDER	136
3.	DYING RACES	142
4.	THE TEXAS RANGER	143
5.	A CLOUD IN THE SKY	148

VIII.

GALVESTON.

1.	A BUFFALO HUNT	154
2.	THE BLUE AND THE GRAY	158
3.	HOME AGAIN	163

IX.

THIRTY YEARS.

THIRTY YEARS 167

X.

TEXAS.

FROM THE DOME OF THE CAPITOL 174

MAIN DOOR OF MISSION SAN JOSÉ, SAN ANTONIO.

UNDER SIX FLAGS.

I.

FORT ST. LOUIS.

(1685-1721.)

1. IN THE NAME OF FRANCE.

ONE morning early in the year 1684, Robert Cavalier, Sieur de la Salle, a gentleman in the King's service, stood waiting in an antechamber of the royal palace at Versailles (Ver-sälz'). Behind the closed door, which was guarded by two of the King's Musketeers in their showy uniforms, his Majesty Louis the Fourteenth was giving a private audience to the Count de Frontenac. This gentleman, late the governor of New France (Canada), was the friend and adviser of *The Adventurer*, as La Salle had been mockingly nicknamed by the idlers of the French court.

La Salle, who was headstrong and somewhat overbearing in character, more used, moreover, to command than to obey, frowned as he walked up and down the room, and glanced impatiently from time to time towards the king's cabinet, where his fate hung in the balance. Months had passed since he had arrived in France from North America, with a great scheme already planned, and lacking only the consent of the king and his ministers. He had danced attendance at court until he was weary, rugged soldier that he was; now filled with hope when the ministers plied him with false promises, now sunk in despair when his enemies placed obstacles in his way. "Would I were back in the wilds of America, with Tonti of the Iron Hand and my red brothers," he muttered, downcast and discouraged.

But at length the door opened, the tapestry was pushed aside, and Frontenac appeared. His eyes beamed with satisfaction. "Your application is granted," he said, pressing La Salle's hand. "His Majesty commissions you to plant a colony at the mouth of the great river where you have already raised the flag of France. Go, my friend; thank his gracious Majesty, and then hasten your preparations for departure."

La Salle.

La Salle lost no time in obeying these directions. His heart throbbed with pride and satisfied ambition. For this was his dream: to colonize the beautiful wilderness watered by the lower Mississippi; to found a city on the banks of the mighty stream whose mouth it had been his good fortune to discover.

But this dream was never to be realized by him. It was the destiny of La Salle not to colonize Louisiana, but to become the discoverer of Texas.

After much trouble La Salle succeeded in perfecting the arrangements for his voyage. His little fleet was composed of four vessels: the *Aimable* (Ā-mah'-bl), the *Joli* (Zho-leé), the *Belle*, and the *St. Francis*. In these embarked over three hundred souls, including women, workmen, priests, and soldiers.

FORT ST. LOUIS.

They sailed from Rochelle, France, on the 24th of July, 1684. The passage across the Atlantic was tedious and stormy; it was embittered by constant quarrels between La Salle and Beaujeu (Bo-zhuh'), the naval commandant of the squadron; and the fleet was crippled by the loss of the *St. Francis*, the store-ship, which was captured by the Spaniards. But toward the end of September the remaining vessels, in tolerable condition, entered the Gulf of Mexico. Here La Salle began a sharp lookout for the wide mouth of the river he aimed to enter.

He was full of confidence in himself, for he had spent years of his life tracking the savage wilderness of the north with his Indian guides, and he had the keen eye and the ready memory of the practiced scout.

But he had no exact chart of the pathless and unknown waters around him; the calculation of the experienced landsman stood him in little stead at sea. He lost his way, and sailing to the westward of the river known to us as the Mississippi, — but called by La Salle the St. Louis, — he came, on the 1st of January, 1685, in sight of the low-lying shores of Texas.

Some weeks later, the fleet anchored in the Gulf outside

The Flag of France.

the beautiful land-locked bay of San Bernard (now Matagorda Bay); and La Salle, flag in hand, and attended by soldiers and priests, set foot on the new land, taking formal possession of it in the name of the King of France.

To the colonists, so long confined within the small ships and overwearied by the monotony of the voyage, it was a joy simply to feast their eyes on the green of the trees that lined the shore, and to breathe the fresh air that blew down, flower-scented, from the far western prairies. They longed to run like children on the sandy beach, to feel under their feet the firm turf. But La Salle's experience among the Indians had taught him caution. He took the utmost care in landing his colonists, and in forming his temporary camps. Two temporary camps were established, one on Matagorda Island, where the lighthouse now stands; the other on the mainland, near the present site of Indianola.

His own heart, meantime, was heavy. He had missed his coveted and beloved river, though he still believed that the San Bernard Bay might be one of its mouths. The *Aimable*, in attempting to enter the harbor, had grounded upon a sandbank and gone to pieces. The Indians, who had swarmed to the coast in great numbers to greet the pale-faced strangers, had already become troublesome. They had, indeed, murdered two of the colonists, named Ory and Desloges. This was the first European blood shed upon Texas soil. The stock of provisions was running low, and finally, to crown all, Beaujeu, from the beginning hostile to La Salle, had hoisted sail, with scant warning, and returned to France, leaving the eight cannons and the powder belonging to the expedition, but carrying away with him all the cannon balls.

A less sturdy spirit might have been wholly disheartened; but La Salle, whatever he felt, gave no signs of weakness. He explored the country round about, and at the end of a short time he marked out the foundation of a fort beside a small stream which empties into the bay. He called the river *Les Vaches* (Cow River[1]), from the number of buffaloes which grazed along the banks. The spot[2] chosen for the site of the fort was a delightful one; the rolling prairies which stretched away northward were covered with rich grass and studded

---

[1] Called by the Spaniards, La Vaca.
[2] Now Dimmitt's Point on the La Vaca.

with belts of noble timber; southward lay the grey and misty line of the bay; birds of gay plumage sang in shadow of the grapevines that trailed from overhanging trees to the water's edge; the clear stream reflected the blue and cloudless sky of southern Texas. Here the colonists set to work. La Salle with his own hands aided in hewing and laying the heavy beams of wall and of blockhouse. The curious savages, tall Lipans and scowling Carankawaes, hung about the place, peering forward with jealous eyes, and picking off the unwary workmen with their deadly arrows. But a day came at last when the little fortress, with its chapel, lodgings, and guardhouse, was completed. Amid the cheers of the colonists the flag of France loosened its folds to the wind; a hymn of thanksgiving and praise arose from the chapel; and La Salle, giving to the fort the name of St. Louis, dedicated it to France in the name of the King.

Several expeditions followed, in 1685 and 1686, the building of Fort St. Louis. La Salle not only cherished the hope of finding his lost river; he was lured northwestward by rumors obtained from the Cenis, the Nassonites, and other friendly Indians, of rich silver mines in the interior. He wished also to communicate, if possible, with his old friend, the Chevalier Tonti of the Iron Hand, whom he had left with a colony on the Illinois River. Tonti, having lost a hand in battle, used one made of iron; hence his title.

These journeys were both painful and perilous; the footsore explorers were obliged to swim swollen rivers; they traversed dangerous swamps and unknown forests; they encountered and fought with hostile Indians; they suffered the pangs of hunger and thirst; they were shaken with chills and parched with fever. It is marvelous, indeed, that a spark of courage should have remained in their hearts.

On returning to the fort after one of these expeditions, during which the commandant had lain for months helpless with fever in the lodge of a Cenis chief, he found matters there in a bad way. The last remaining vessel, the *Belle*, had been wrecked on a shoal in the bay. Food was scarce; ammunition was almost exhausted; and between death from sickness and losses in Indian skirmishes, the inmates were reduced to less than forty persons.

La Salle's Map of Texas.

Despite all this, however, as the wayworn explorers drew near the walls, their ears were greeted with sounds of mirth and revelry. The Sieur Barbier and "one of the maidens"—as the chronicler relates — had just been married in the little chapel. The wedding party welcomed their chief with joyous shouts. We can well imagine how, removing his worn cap, he saluted the youthful pair with a stately bow. And the same evening, when the colonists gathered in the log-built hall of the commandant's own quarters to make merry over the first European wedding on Texas soil, with what courtly grace did the Sieur de la Salle tread a measure with the blushing bride!

This was in October, 1686. On the 12th of January the following year, La Salle appeared in the open square of the Fort, dressed in his faded red uniform and equipped for traveling. His people pressed around him, listening with anxious hearts to his farewell words. For he was about starting once more across vast and unknown regions in search of Tonti — and help.

One by one he called to his side those whom he had chosen to accompany him. They numbered twenty — exactly half of the remnant of his colony. Among them were two of his own nephews and his brother, Cavalier; the faithful priest, Father Anastase; Joutel, the young historian of the colony; Liotot (Lee-o-to); L'Archevêque (Larsh-vāke'); Duhaut (Du-ho'); and Nika (Nee-ka), an Indian hunter who had followed La Salle to France from Canada.

Sieur Barbier was placed in command of the garrison; and, after an affectionate farewell, La Salle passed through the gate, which he was never to enter again, and plunged a last time into the forest.

Two months later, near the crossing of the Neches River, Moragnet (Mo-rä-nyā), La Salle's nephew, who had been for some time on bad terms with L'Archevêque and Duhaut, was murdered by them while he was sleeping. Nika, who was with the party (which had been sent out after fresh buffalo meat), was killed at the same time. The murderers, fearful of La Salle's just vengeance, determined to take his life also. They placed themselves in ambush; L'Archevêque, who was only sixteen years old, was detailed to lead their chief into the trap.

When La Salle appeared, in search of his nephew, he was fired upon and instantly killed (March 16, 1687).

Thus perished, by treacherous hands, the gallant and stouthearted La Salle — the soldier, explorer, and dreamer. He was buried in the lonely spot where he fell. Father Anastase scooped out a shallow grave for his friend and benefactor, and pressed the grassy turf upon his breast. And so, within the borders of Texas — though the exact spot is unknown — repose the mortal remains of its discoverer.

Joutel with several of the band succeeded after many adventures in reaching one of Tonti's settlements on the Arkansas River. Thence they made their way to Canada.

The assassins and their followers remained with the Indians, where, one after another, they nearly all met the same bloody and violent death they had meted out to their victims.

Five years later L'Archevêque with one companion was recaptured by the Spaniards from the savages and sent to Madrid.[1]

Tonti of the Iron Hand had waited long and anxiously for news of his friend. In 1684 he had gone in a canoe down the Mississippi to its mouth to meet the expedition from France. The expedition did not appear, and he returned to his post on the upper Mississippi. He questioned the Indian runners from the south and west as they passed his camp on their hunting raids. He could learn nothing of La Salle or his companions. That intrepid captain seemed to have vanished into the unknown west. At last, in 1689, he journeyed southward again in quest of his friend. Vague rumors reached him of men who had passed through his own forts and tarried to tell the story of La Salle's death. But he would not believe them. He entered Texas and traveled as far as the wigwams of the friendly Cenis. From them he learned the fate of the man he loved; and the rugged soldier turned aside his head and wept.[2]

---

[1] L'Archevêque afterward returned to America and settled in Santa Fé, New Mexico, where he married and died, and where his descendants still live. See A. F. Bandelier's *Gilded Man*.

La Salle never married. His title was inherited by his brother, numerous descendants of whom are living in Louisiana.

2. IN THE NAME OF SPAIN.

While these things were taking place in an obscure corner of the New World, there was commotion in the court of Spain. Word had come over from the "Golden West" that France had laid an unlawful hand upon some of the Spanish possessions there. Letters flew thick and fast between the Spanish viceroy in Mexico and the Spanish king's[1] ministers. The viceroy was ordered to punish the offenders as soon as ever they could be found; the dark-browed king of Spain was very angry.

All this stir was caused by the capture of the *St. Francis*, La Salle's little store-ship in 1684. She was plainly on her way to some new colony. But where had that colony been planted? The wary captain of the *St. Francis* said that he did not know. Perhaps he told the truth. At any rate, it was not until 1686 and after a world of trouble that the viceroy in Mexico located the spot of La Salle's settlement. Spain considered herself at that time the legitimate owner of all that region which we now call Texas; she pretended, indeed, to own everything bordering on the Gulf of Mexico. A military council was therefore held at the new post of Monclova, and Captain Alonzo de Leon, the newly appointed governor of Coaquila (afterwards called Coahuila) (Co-ah-wee'-la), was dispatched to find and destroy La Salle and his colony. La Salle, with a bullet in his brain, had been lying for two years in his shallow grave near the Neches River; but the viceroy did not know this.

Captain De Leon and his hundred soldiers marched gaily and confidently from Monclova in a northeasterly direction, across wild prairie and savage woodland. They were used to the ways of the Comanches, through whose hunting grounds they marched, and, at need, could take scalp for scalp; they were well fed and comfortably clad; the King's pay jingled in

---

[1] Charles II.

their pockets, — a brave contrast truly to the starved, ragged, disheartened colonists at Fort St. Louis!

But when Captain De Leon and his men at length found the fort, the unfortunate French colonists, like their chief, had perished. Their bleaching bones lay scattered about the door of the blockhouse, where they had made their last desperate stand against the bloodthirsty Carankawaes. De Leon's heart stirred with pity as he looked about him, thinking less, perhaps, of the men — for it is a soldier's business to die — than of the delicate women who had shared their fate.

With the Cenis, into whose friendly wigwams they had escaped at the time of the massacre, De Leon found several of the colonists. These were afterwards sent back to their homes in France. But among them there is no mention of the Sieur Barbier and his young bride.

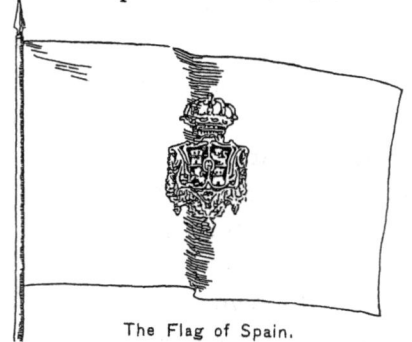

The Flag of Spain.

De Leon, it is said, — though this is a much disputed fact, — called the country about Fort St. Louis Texas, because of his kindly treatment by the Cenis Indians, the word *Texas* in their tongue meaning friends.[1] On his return to Monclova, he pictured this Texas as a paradise so fertile and so beautiful that the viceroy determined to establish there a mission and presidio, — that is to say, a church and stronghold, — for the double purpose of reducing and converting the Indians.

In 1690 Captain De Leon, with several priests added to his company of soldiers, marched again to Fort St. Louis. The broken walls were restored, and once more the air rang with the cheerful sounds of axe and hammer. The Mission of San

---

[1] The name more probably was derived from the Tehas Indians, a tribe whose central village was built on the present site of Mound Prairie.

Francisco was begun and dedicated; the Spanish flag fluttered in the breeze; a hymn of praise and thanksgiving arose from the chapel; and De Leon took formal possession of the country in the name of the King of Spain.

The Spaniards, harried by the Indians and too far from Monclova to receive regular supplies, were soon forced to abandon Fort St. Louis. Great was the rejoicing among the Lipans and the Carankawaes when the pale faces disappeared from among them, leaving the bay once more free to their own canoes, the prairies open to their moccasined feet.

Neither France nor Spain for a time seemed inclined to trouble herself further about this disputed property.

But in 1719 a French ship bound for the Mississippi drifted, like La Salle's fleet, westward to the bay of San Bernard. Among those who went ashore for recreation, while the sailors were taking on fresh water, were Monsieur Belleisle, a French officer, and four of his friends. They did not reappear at the appointed signal, and the captain, after waiting for them for some hours, sailed away without them.

Belleisle and his companions were in despair at finding themselves thus abandoned; they wandered for weeks along the strange and lonely coast, living, as best they could, upon roots, berries, and insects. Finally four of the men died of starvation, leaving Belleisle alone. Weak and despairing, he made his way to the interior, where he soon fell into the hands of some Indians, whom he took at first to be cannibals. They stripped him and divided his clothing among themselves; but instead of eating him, as he expected they would do, they gave him to an old woman of the tribe, who made him her slave but who otherwise treated him with rude kindness. In time he learned the language of his captors and became a warrior, sometimes even leading their savage forays.

One day an embassy from another tribe came to the camp. Belleisle, listening to their talk, heard the name of St. Denis.

Now St. Denis was one of his own former comrades-in-arms. Belleisle's heart leaped. He wrote, with ink made of soot, a few lines on his officer's commission, — which he had somehow kept, — and secretly bribed one of the strange Indians to carry this message to St. Denis. St. Denis happened at the time to be at Natchitoches (Nack-ee-tosh) beyond the Sabine River; when he read the note he was much affected. He immediately sent horses, arms, and clothing to the captive; Belleisle, by means of a strategy, escaped with the Indian guides and joined his friend.

This adventure of Monsieur Belleisle caused him later to become a part of the history of Fort St. Louis.

3. IN THE NAME OF OBLIVION.

The unfortunate La Salle had died with his ardent and long-cherished dream unfulfilled. But after more than thirty years, another man had begun to realize that dream. Jean Baptiste Le Moyne, Sieur de Bienville had sailed with French ships up the beloved river; his colonists were fast peopling the beautiful wilderness, and already the infant city of New Orleans lay strong and thriving on the bank of the Mississippi.

The commandant of Louisiana, though busied with his growing colony, kept yet a watchful eye upon the grasping Spaniards, who claimed the country eastward nearly to the Mississippi. But France claimed westward as far as the bay of San Bernard, by virtue of La Salle's discovery. Bienville determined to make good the claim of France. In August, 1721, he fitted out a small vessel, the *Subtile*, told off a detachment of tried soldiers, and placed Bernard de la Harpe, an experienced captain, in command. The expedition set out at once to recover La Salle's old fort. Belleisle, on account of his knowledge of the country and the Indian language, was sent along as guide.

The surprise and the rage of the Indians when they saw the hated flag waving again above the fort may be imagined. They threw themselves with such fury against the newcomers that La Harpe, seeing his small garrison in danger of massacre, withdrew quietly, and returned in October to New Orleans.

Fort St. Louis was left at last to a solitude never again to be broken. Vines grew over the crumbling walls and sprawled across the floors where human feet had passed; lizards basked in crevices of the blockhouse; and wild creatures from the wood took up their abode in the chapel. Day by day and year by year decay and change went on, until there came a time when nothing remained to tell of the place where the first settlers of Texas lived, suffered, rejoiced, and perished.

II.

SAN ANTONIO.

(1714-1794.)

1. A BOLD RIDER.

IN 1714 Juchereau St. Denis rode across Texas, in an oblique line from a trading post in Louisiana to a presidio on the Rio Grande River. This was the same St. Denis who afterward, as already related, rescued his comrade-in-arms Belleisle from captivity. He had secret orders from Cadillac, the governor of Louisiana, and his busy brain was teeming with carefully laid plans of his own. His escort consisted of twelve white men and two or three Indians. He took his bearings as he went, carefully marking the way from river to river, from prairie to forest, from Indian village to buffalo range; thus sketching out that long thoroughfare which afterwards became famous as the "Old San Antonio Road."

Much of the way lay through the lands of unfriendly Indians; but St. Denis rode as jauntily as if the men at his back were a thousand instead of a dozen.

And when one day he drew rein on the brow of a certain hill, and gazed down into the lovely cup-like valley where a few huts marked the beginnings of San Antonio, he might, for all signs of fatigue upon his handsome young face, have just quitted the governor's residence.

"A beautiful site for a city," he said to Jallot, his confidential servant. His pleased eyes roved over the smiling valley, through which the river ran like a silver thread. Graceful trees lined the river banks; the tender grass was studded with a thousand flowers of varied colors; there was a life-giving softness in the wind that came from the low mountains to the northward.

St. Denis journeyed on to St. John the Baptist, carrying this lovely picture in his heart as he went. St. John the Baptist was a presidio on the Rio Grande River. It was built by Captain Alonzo de Leon, after his return from Fort St. Louis in 1689. Its commandant, at the time of the visit of St. Denis, was Don Pedro de Villescas. To Don Pedro St. Denis unfolded his mission — the opening of trade between Louisiana and Mexico. The friendly commandant could do nothing without first consulting his superiors; so he asked St. Denis to wait until a letter could be sent to the governor of the province at Monclova. St. Denis waited, and while he was waiting he fell in love with Donna Maria, the commandant's daughter.

The young French officer was so dashing, so courtly, and withal so good looking, that it is no wonder Don Pedro's daughter loved him in return; and there were at least two very happy persons at the Presidio of St. John the Baptist.

But when the courier came back from Monclova, St. Denis was seized by order of the governor, and was carried under guard to that city.

The governor of Coahuila was, as it happened, a rejected suitor of Donna Maria Villescas. Filled with jealous rage, he threw the young Frenchman into prison and threatened him with death unless he would give up all claim to his promised bride.

This St. Denis gallantly refused to do. After some months the governor sent him to the city of Mexico, denouncing him to the viceroy as a spy against the government. He was again placed in prison, where he was treated with great severity.

Donna Maria, however, was not idle all this time. She had sent several spirited letters to the governor at Monclova, and she now wrote to the viceroy himself. Her letter had the effect of loosening the chains of her lover.

Marquis de Linares, the viceroy, when he saw his prisoner, was so charmed that he offered the young Frenchman an important post in the Spanish army. But St. Denis would not consent to abandon his own flag. The viceroy then gave him a handsome horse, and parting from him with regret, sent him back to the presidio, where he married the loyal Donna Maria.

Before leaving the presidio on his return to Louisiana, he made secret arrangements for smuggling goods into Mexico.

The viceroy, having a hint of this, did not trouble St. Denis again; but he decided to establish posts and missions throughout the New Philippines — as Texas was still called — with garrisons armed to prevent contraband trade. Captain Domingo Ramon was appointed to carry on this work. He set out at once from St. John the Baptist for San Antonio, with a company of soldiers and several friars under his command. St. Denis, in high spirits and sure of his own success in spite of Captain Ramon, rode with him, acting as his guide.

2. COWL AND CARBINE.

Mission and presidio, as already stated, meant church and fortress. The places chosen for these buildings were generally in the very midst of populous and fierce Indian tribes. For the object of the builders was not only to hold the country against France, but also to reduce the savages and convert them to the Catholic religion.

The Red Man had already his own rude belief in the Great Spirit who sat behind the clouds and watched over the flight of his arrows and the tasseling of his corn. He loved to tell about the Happy Hunting-grounds to which he would travel after death, attended by his horse and his dog.

It required a great deal of patience and perseverance on the part of the missionaries to make these wild creatures understand the meaning of the strange things they saw and heard:

the hymns and prayers which broke the stillness at morning and at eventide, the candles blazing on the altar, the tinkling of bells, the movements of the priests, the humble attitude of the proud Spanish soldiers at mass. They crowded about the chapels, now accepting the new faith with childlike confidence, at other times seeking a chance to massacre priest and soldier in cold blood.

But these missionaries belonged to an order whose business it was to be patient. They were Franciscans from the monastery of St. Francis at Zacatecas in Mexico, and they were pledged to poverty and self-denial. Gentle, but sturdy, these barefooted friars, in their coarse woolen frocks and rope girdles, exercised a strange fascination over the Indians who fell under their influence.

Captain Domingo Ramon went bravely to work with his

A Franciscan Father.

soldiers and Franciscans. He was very much loved by the Indians. They adopted him into their tribes and cheerfully aided him in the hard labor of clearing and building. Within a few years the country was dotted with missions. Some of these were temporary structures, rude and frail; others were built of stone. The noble and majestic ruins of the latter fill the beholder to-day with wonder and delight. If the mission served also as a presidio, it was entitled to a garrison of two hundred and fifty soldiers; where there was no fortress, the church itself served as a stronghold. Among the earliest of the missions thus built were Our Lady of Guadalupe (Gwah-dah-loop'ā), at Victoria (1714); Mission Orquizacas (Or-kee-sa'-kass), on the San Jacinto River (1715); Mission Dolores, near San Augustine (1716); Adaes, east of the Sabine River (1718); Nacogdoches (1715); and Espiritu Santo, at Goliad (La Bahia) (1718).

The Mission Alamo,[1] which was to play so prominent a part in the later history of Texas, was begun under another name, in 1703, on the Rio Grande River. It was removed to the San Pedro River at San Antonio in 1718. In 1744 it was finally built where its ruins now stand, on the Alamo Plaza in San Antonio, and was called the Church of the Alamo.

Early in 1718 the foundation of San José (Ho-sa') de Aguayo, the largest and finest of all the missions, was laid near San Antonio. The little settlement which had so pleased the eye of St. Denis four years before had grown to a village. It had been laid off and named for the Duke de Bexar (Bair), a viceroy of Mexico; and St. Denis' road, which linked it on the southwest with St. John the Baptist and on the northeast with Natchitoches in Louisiana, had already become a traveled highway. The Mission and Presidio of San José were therefore of the first importance.

Captain Ramon himself may have selected the site. It was a few miles below the town, on the limpid and swift-flowing river San Antonio. A day or two after the site was decided upon, a long procession wound across the beautiful open prairie from the village. It was headed by a venerable barefoot Franciscan father, who carried aloft a large wooden cross; on either side of him walked a friar of the same order, and behind them came acolytes and altar-boys bearing censer, bell, and vessels of holy water. Captain Ramon and his soldiers on horseback, and stiff and erect in their holiday uniforms, followed with the Spanish flag in their midst; the Mexicans who

[1] *Alamo*, cottonwood.

composed the slim population of San Antonio came next; then, grave and stately in their blankets and feathered head-dresses and as proud as the Spaniards themselves, stalked a hundred or more converted Apache and Comanche warriors. A rabble of Indian squaws and papooses brought up the rear.

This procession went slowly along under the morning sun, now over the flower-set prairie, now through a strip of woodland. The river, breast-high to the women and boys, was forded, and as the foremost group reached the farther shore, the old Franciscan lifted his hand; a church hymn, sweet, powerful, resonant, arose from five hundred throats. Thus they came, singing, to the place where San José was to stand.

A large space was marked off; the ground plan of the great church was sketched on the turf, — perhaps with the point of Captain Domingo Ramon's sword; the church prayers were said, and the corner-stone, already hewn and shaped, was sprinkled with holy water.

The scene on the spot daily thereafter for many years was a busy and picturesque one. Everybody worked with a will, — soldiers, priests, and Indians, all filled with a holy zeal. Even the Indian women fetched sand in their aprons, and the Indian children set their small brown bodies against the stones and helped push them into place. Tradition says that the people brought milk from their goats and cows to mix the mortar, thereby making it firmer and more lasting.

The beautiful twin towers went slowly up; the great dome was rounded over the main chapel; the double row of arched cloisters stretched their lovely length along the wall; the artist, Juan Huicar (wee'-car), sent out by the king of Spain, set his fine carvings above the wide doors.

At the same time the enclosing wall was raised; the fort with its flying buttresses, the guardhouse, the huts into which the Indian converts were locked at night — all these were completed. Orchards and gardens were planted, and irrigating ditches were dug. Again and again the work was interrupted by attacks from Indians; but when the fight was over the dead were buried, the wounded were cared for, and the building and planting went on as before.[1]

Such was the manner of the building of the Texas missions. It took sixty years to complete San José. In the meantime the handsome Mission of La Purissima Concepcion (Immaculate Conception) and San Francisco de la Espada (St. Francis of the Sword) were erected, both also on the San Antonio River.

The Mission of San Saba was built in 1734, on the San Saba River in what is now Menard County. The good fathers were at first very successful in converting the Apaches and the Comanches, who flocked to them in great numbers. But the reopening of *Las Almagras* (red ores), an old silver mine near the mission, brought into the neighborhood many reckless men; and quarrels soon arose between them and the Indians — quarrels which were one day to bear bitter fruit.

3. A HURRIED RIDE.

In 1719 St. Denis was at Natchitoches, which was one of the outposts of the French in Louisiana and close to the Texas border. He had traveled back and forth through Texas more than once since his first trip to the presidio on the Rio Grande; and he had spent much of his time in Mexican dungeons. But for that he bore the Spaniards no great ill-will. He had escaped from prison and brought his beautiful Mexican wife away with him; and when he made his flying journeys he turned aside, no doubt, to see his Spanish friend, Captain Domingo Ramon — who, by the way, was his wife's uncle — and to admire the missions which were going up in every direction under that captain's vigorous management. But now things

---

[1] These Spanish and Indian builders were called "The Children of San José."

were changed. A few months before, France and Spain, never on good terms with each other, had declared open war.

St. Denis, if the truth were told, was glad of a chance to fight somebody besides Indians. He was right weary of the skulking ways of the red warrior with his tomahawk, his paint and feathers, and his savage desire to carry scalps at his belt. He longed for a good honest brush with white men. who fought openly with gun and sword — men, for example, like his good friend Captain Ramon and his troop of jolly soldiers!

He leaped lightly into the saddle one morning and galloped out of Natchitoches at the head of a hundred and fifty men. Bernard de la Harpe, in joint command of the expedition, rode by his side.

They crossed the Sabine River and attacked the garrisons at the Missions of Nacogdoches, Aes, and Orquizacas, all of whom, surprised by the sudden onslaught, retreated before them. It was a lively chase across the vast territory, with a good deal of skirmishing; and it ended only when the Spaniards were safe inside the town of San Antonio.

St. Denis, drawing rein on the brow of the hill and gazing down once more into the lovely valley, saw a sort of orderly confusion on an open plaza in the heart of the town; horsemen were gathering, men were moving hurriedly about, and from the midst of the bustle the clear tones of a bell suddenly fell upon the air. It was the call to arms!

St. Denis smiled and turned to La Harpe: "It is high time we were riding homeward," he said gaily, with a glance at their small band of wayworn troopers; and turning their horses' heads they galloped away.

None too soon! For shortly afterwards the Marquis de Aguayo, governor of the province, came out of the town with a fresh troop of five hundred Spaniards, tried soldiers and eager recruits, and galloped in pursuit of the flying Frenchmen. It was another lively chase across the vast territory;

but this time it was France who retreated, with Spain at her heels. Captain Ramon, quite as anxious for a tilt with civilized soldiers as his friendly enemy and nephew-in-law St. Denis, left the work of mission-building in the hands of his friars, and, as second in command, joined the governor-general in this pursuit.

Aguayo, following the example of St. Denis, did not pause until the intruders were safe in their own citadel at Natchitoches; then he replaced at the Missions of Orquizacas and Aes the men whom he had brought back with him, and he left for their protection a stout garrison at the Mission of Nuestra Señora del Pilar (Our Lady of the Font), about twenty miles west of Natchitoches.

He was as keenly alive as St. Denis himself to the natural beauty of the valley watered by the San Pedro and San Antonio Rivers; and on his return to San Antonio he set on foot many improvements, including the widening and deepening of the irrigating ditches.

These irrigating ditches were called *acequias* (a-sa'-kee-a). They are still in use, and many of them are very beautiful. One known as the Acequia Madre, or Mother Ditch, is as deep and wide as a small rivulet; the living waters, pure and cool, rush along a bed lined and parapeted with stone, and overhung with pomegranates and rustling banana leaves.

The water from the ditches is turned, by means of gates, into the fields and gardens which lie along its course. Each landowner is entitled to so much water a day, or at a stated period. This inflow of the crystal flood is called the *saca de agua* (taking the water), and is hailed with delight as it comes singing its way through corn-row, garden-patch, and rose-bower.

In the early days the completing of a water-ditch was celebrated as a feast. Rows of cactus were planted on its banks to keep off cattle, and shade-trees were set out along its course.

A priest, attended by acolytes, blessed the water. The following day a drum was beaten at morning mass, and all those who had contributed in money or labor to the making of the ditch were summoned to the church to take part in the Suerte (soo-air'-ta), — a lottery for the drawing of the land watered by the new sluice. Tickets were placed in an urn and were drawn out by two children. The lucky holders of the highest numbers got the best lands. At night, by way of winding up the feast, there would be a procession and a *fandango*[1] on the plaza.

The good Marquis de Aguayo further recommended to the Spanish government at Madrid to send colonists to the province. "One family," he said, "is better than a hundred soldiers."

Then, having done all he could for the New Philippines, he went back to his official residence at Monclova, attended as far as St. John the Baptist by Captain Ramon.

4. INDIOS BRAVOS.

The Spanish government, acting on the governor-general's advice, ordered four hundred families to be sent out to the New Philippines from the Canary Islands. These islands, situated off the coast of Africa, belonged to Spain by right of conquest, and were settled by Spaniards of pure blood, noted for their honor and chastity, and for their devotion to the Catholic religion. Of the four hundred families only thirteen ever came. They reached San Antonio by way of Mexico in 1729, bringing with them their stores of clothing, silverware, and jewels. They built their dwellings around the present square of the Constitution, which they called *Plaza de las Islas* (Square of the Islands), in homesick memory of the sea-girt isles they had left behind.

[1] A Mexican dance.

Other colonists from Monterey and from Lake Teztuco, in Mexico, followed; houses sprung up beside the musical water-ways; vines were trained over the yellow adobe walls; semi-tropical vegetation made a paradise of the spreading fields and gardens. Finally, the newcomers, emulous of the growing walls of San José, laid on their plaza the foundation (1731) of San Fernando Church.

Enlarged and rebuilt on the same spot, San Fernando remains to this day the parish church of the Spanish-speaking Catholics of San Antonio.

But the settlers, or townspeople — as they may now be called — were full of anxiety in those troublous times. No more French soldiers, it is true, came riding across the border, chasing the Spanish troops to their very gates. But there were the Apaches and the Comanches. For in spite of the efforts of Spanish friars and Spanish soldiers, but few of the Apaches and Comanches had become *Indios reducidos* (converted Indians). Thousands of *Indios bravos* (wild Indians), as savage and cruel as if a mission had never been built, roamed the country, ready to swoop down at any moment upon the ill-guarded little post. A messenger would hurry in, perhaps from the missions below, which kept ever a keen lookout, breathless with the news that the Apaches were creeping stealthily upon the town. Or, suddenly and without warning, a ringing war-whoop would echo in the air, and leaping from cover to cover among the scattered houses, the Comanches, tomahawk in hand, would pursue their hapless victims to some last hiding-place; then, leaving death and desolation behind, they would vanish as suddenly as they had come.

At last the new settlers determined to put an end to this state of affairs. They organized themselves into a small army, and aided by the little garrison of soldiers then stationed there, they marched against their Indian foes, whom they defeated in a pitched battle.

This victory (in 1732) gave some security to the place. The *Indios bravos* still harried the country, killing those who ventured far from post and mission, and plundering where they could not kill. A number of years later (1752), after a fresh quarrel with the miners at Las Almagras, they fell upon the Mission of San Saba, and butchered every human creature within its walls. But rarely did they again venture near the dwellings of those determined pale-faces who had overcome them on their own hunting-grounds.

5. ALONG THE OLD SAN ANTONIO ROAD.

The years drifted on, peaceful and sluggish, towards the end of the eighteenth century. There were few happenings either in San Antonio itself or in the province, which was at last laid down on the map as Texas. There was no further dispute concerning boundary lines or property. Spain was the lawful owner of everything west of the Mississippi River. For Louis the Fifteenth of France, in 1762, for state reasons, presented to the King of Spain the handsome French province of Louisiana. The people of Louisiana were very angry when they learned — more than a year after the transfer — that they had been handed over without their knowledge or consent to the hated Spaniard. But Louis did not trouble himself in the least about what they thought or felt. Thus, the colonists being all Spanish subjects, were bound to peace among themselves. Even the dashing St. Denis, had he lived so long, could have found nobody to fight except the despised Indian. But that doughty warrior and courtly gentleman had long since fired his last shot on the field, and trod his last measure in the dance. According to the old chroniclers he remained to the end of his life "a devoted friend and a noble fighter."

In 1729 a widespread plot was formed among the Indians in Texas and Louisiana to massacre all white people within reach, Spanish and French, men, women, and children. A friendly chief warned St. Denis of the plot. He gathered his troopers hastily together and rode out of Natchitoches, where he had continued in command, and in a short time defeated

The Cathedral of San Fernando.

and scattered the tribes. After this they hated and feared him, but they looked upon him with awe, believing him to be protected by their own Manitou.

He was at length killed by the chief of the Natchez Indians. He lies buried near the town of Natchitoches.

In spite of the peace between Spain and France (1762) — or perhaps because of it — there was little progress in Texas. Spain forbade her colonists to trade with other nations; she did not allow them to manufacture anything that could be made in the mother-country, or to plant anything that could with profit be sent over from there. They were even forbidden to trade with their fellow-colonists in Louisiana.[1] Under these hard conditions settlers came in slowly. Texas remained almost neglected, peopled only by fierce savages.

But the little town in the southwest had a life of its own. Nearly everybody who had any business with Texas or Mexico traveled the Old San Antonio Road laid out by St. Denis in 1714; and all travelers halted at this lovely oasis in the wilderness. They were always loth to go away. For there were wonderful *fiestas* (feasts) in the Churches of the Alamo and San Fernando, and solemn processions to the grand Missions of Concepcion and San José; there were stately gatherings in the houses of the Island Spaniards, and merry boating parties on the blue-green waters of the river San Antonio. There were gay dances on the plaza at night to the music of guitar and castanet, and Mexican jugglers throwing balls and knives by the light of smoking torches. Bands of Mexican muleteers jingled in from the presidio on the Rio Grande, driving before them trains of mules loaded with ingots of silver, on their way to Natchitoches, four hundred miles distant; caravans traveling westward with bales of smuggled goods crawled lazily through the narrow streets. There was a continued coming and going of swarthy soldiers and black-gowned priests, governors, bishops, alcades, and christianized Indians; among them appeared, now and then, the fair face and wiry form of the American, the forerunner of that race which was one day to sweep all the others out of its path and to possess the land.

Once, in 1779, when Spain and England were at war with each other, there was even more than the usual stir on the Military Plaza. Nearly all the inhabitants of the town were gathered about the doors of the Church of the Alamo, where a

---

[1] Salcedo, the Spanish commander at Monterey, said that if " he had the power he would stop even the birds from flying across the Sabine."

priest was saying mass. Presently there was a burst of martial music, and a little company of soldiers came out ; their heads were lifted proudly and their step was firm and assured. A cheer broke forth from the crowd ; the soldiers sent back an answering shout as they mounted their waiting horses and rode away under the gaudy pennon of Leon and Castile.

Spain was at this time at war with England, and this handful of fighting men was the quota of troops furnished by the Spanish province of Texas to Don Galvez, the commander-in-chief of the army at New Orleans. They reached Louisiana in time to take an active part in the war and to rejoice with Galvez over his victories at Natchez, Mobile, and Pensacola.

In 1794 all the missions were secularized; that is, the control of them was taken away from the priests and given to the civil authorities. Upon this, the Missions of San José and Concepcion ceased to be the centers of activity they had been for nearly a century. San Antonio was shorn of a part of her glory. The majestic buildings remained, but the pomp and circumstance of fortress and chapel had forever departed.

III.

NACOGDOCHES.

(1794-1821.)

1. A FATAL VENTURE.

ONE of the earliest missions planned by Captain Ramon was that of Our Lady of Nacogdoches (1715). It was built on the lands of the Naugodoches Indians, not far from the disputed boundary of Texas, and nearly on a line with the French post of Natchitoches in Louisiana. Some priests, whose duty it was to convert the Indians, were placed there, and with them a small garrison of Spanish soldiers to watch the French at Natchitoches. This was one of those garrisons surprised in 1718 by St. Denis, and driven to the gates of San Antonio. The soldiers were brought back and reinstated by Aguayo; and from that time on, to the close of the century, the little military post was kept up.

Monsieur de Pagès, a French gentleman who in 1766 passed across Texas on a voyage around the world, received from the missionary fathers at Aes, Adaes, and Nacogdoches a hospitable welcome. He describes particularly the Mission of "Naquadock" (Nacogdoches) with its "plaza and its pleasant trees," and says that the "half-savage Spanish soldiers" at the presidio, when they were upon their horses, recalled to his mind the ancient chevaliers. The Spanish "bold-rider" wore a cuirass of antelope skin and carried a shield, a large sword, a carbine, and a pair of pistols. His arms and the equipment of his horse were very heavy and cumbersome, but he was an "amazing good fighter." Monsieur de Pagès, who was an officer in the French navy, was also a correspondent of the Academy of Sciences at Paris. He took careful notes in all the countries through which he passed. He describes the soil and climate of Texas and the animals, especially the fine, robust horses. "A good horse," he says, "may be had for a pair of shoes." But his greatest interest is in the savages. He mentions the Comanches, the Apaches, the Adaes, and the

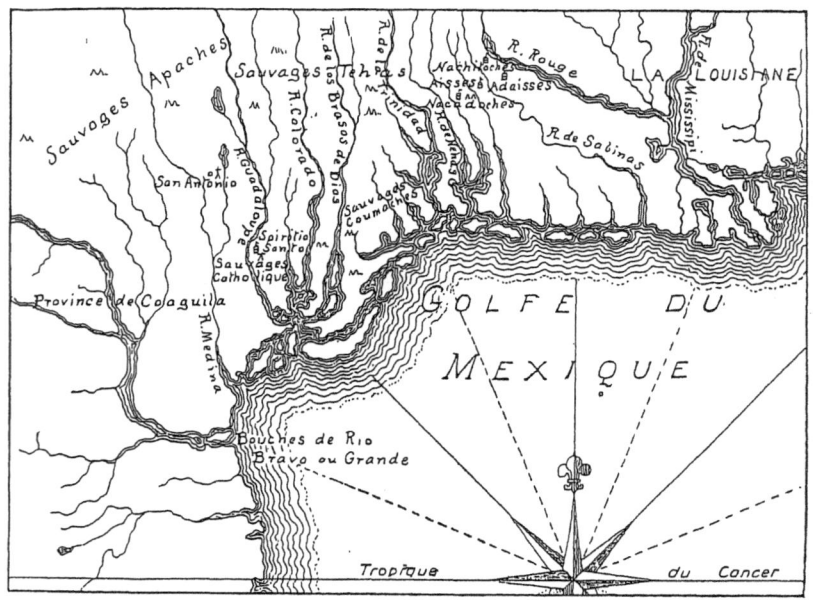

De Pagès' Map of Texas.

Tehas tribes. The Tehas, he says, were a "corn-growing people." He spent some time at the Mission of Nacogdoches ("Naquadock") in company with a deposed governor of the province.

In 1778 a stone fort, which still stands, was built at Nacogdoches by Captain Gil Y Barbo for the accommodation of the Spanish soldiers. A few huts were clustered about the presidio, for it was on the Old San Antonio Road and was a stopping-place for travelers; but it was a dull and lonely spot.

Suddenly, with the birth of a new century, it awoke from its long slumber and became, in a way, the starting-point of Texas history. It was the gateway through which Anglo-American energy and ambition came in to Texas. From its plaza unrolled a panorama full of life and vigor: scenes in which adventurers, freebooters, patriots, and dreamers played their parts.

The panorama opens with Philip Nolan.

Philip Nolan, a young man of Irish descent, obtained in 1797 a permit from De Nava, the Spanish commandant-general of Texas, to collect in that province wild horses for the American army. He entered the province, made friends with the Indians, and succeeded in gathering twelve hundred mustangs, which he drove across the border. He drew and brought back with him at this time a map of Texas, the first one ever made. This map he gave to Baron Carondelet, the Spanish governor at New Orleans.[1]

Three years later, with the same permit and ostensibly on the same errand, he started westward from Natchez, Mississippi. He had with him seventeen white men and one negro. His second in command was a nineteen-year-old lad named Ellis Bean. The men were all young, most of them being under thirty and many of them hardly more than twenty years of age.

They traveled on horseback across the wilderness, and some months later they encamped in the neighborhood of the present city of Waco, where they found "elk and deer plenty, some buffalo, and thousands of wild horses."[2] In a short time they had caught and penned three hundred mustangs. The Indians were very friendly. At one time two hundred Comanches vis-

---

[1] Nolan afterward claimed to have made this map for the benefit of the United States government in case of a war with Spain. He wrote, upon the eve of this journey: "Will we have a war? At all events, I can cut my way back and you can rely upon me." (Letter to General Wilkinson, June 10, 1797.) [2] Ellis Bean's diary.

ited them in their camp. In return they spent a month in the wigwams of that tribe. Then they went back to their business of capturing wild horses.

But orders in the meantime had come from De Nava to Musquiz, the Spanish captain at Nacogdoches, to arrest Nolan at all hazards. He had been denounced to the Spanish government as a traitor, and it was believed that he had come to Texas for the purpose of setting up a republic of his own, or to further the plans of Aaron Burr.[1]

Ellis P. Bean.

Musquiz left Nacogdoches on the 4th of March, 1801, with one hundred soldiers, in search of the supposed conspirator. After a few days' march he sent for El Blanco, a famous Indian chief, and offered him a large bribe if he would lead him to Nolan's camp. El Blanco proudly spurned this base offer. Some Indian spies, however, served as guides, and at daybreak on the 22d of March Musquiz found the camp. He attacked Nolan and his men, who returned his fire from their rude blockhouse. Nolan, whose rifle had been stolen from him by a deserter from his own camp, was killed in a few moments. Bean took command and the fighting went on desperately for some time. Finally, on a promise from the Spaniards that they should be set free as soon as they reached Nacogdoches, the outnumbered Americans surrendered. They buried their gallant leader, whose dream of a republic, if he had one, died with

[1] Burr at this time was suspected of a design to separate the southwestern states from the Union and found a new government.

him; and they set out with their captors for the Presidio of Nacogdoches. There, instead of the promised freedom, they found chains and captivity. They were heavily ironed and placed in close confinement. At the end of a month they were marched into the plaza, bound together, two and two. There was a beating of drums and a fluttering of Spanish pennons. The hearts of the poor young prisoners beat high with hope. Knowing that they had been guilty of no crime, they seemed already to feel their chains falling off, and they laughed joyfully, lifting their pallid faces to the free blue sky. But a harsh voice gave the order " Forward March !" and driven by brutal guards they limped painfully away to Mexican dungeons.

It was six years before the King of Spain found time to sentence these prisoners. A royal decree then came (1807) ordering every fifth man to be shot. By this time but nine were left alive, and the officer in charge decided that one only should suffer death.

The nine wretched captives threw dice to determine which of their number should die. The lot fell to Ephraim Blackburn, the oldest man among them. He was executed without delay.

Only one of the others ever breathed the blessed air of freedom again. Ellis Bean, after many strange and thrilling adventures, finally escaped. His companions, to a man, perished in loathsome Mexican prisons, some of them within a short time, others after a wretched captivity of more than fifteen years, — all ignorant to the last of the cause of their imprisonment.

2. THE DISPUTED BOUNDARY LINE.

While Nacogdoches was rubbing her sleepy eyes and staring at the *Americanos*, who kept coming into Texas in spite of the scant welcome they got there, a man was strutting about the court at Madrid in Spain, carrying Texas, so to speak, in his pocket. Manuel de Godoy, called *El Principe de la Paz* (The

Prince of the Peace), who, from a private in the King's Guards, had come to be a grandee of Spain and first minister of the King's council, was a corrupt courtier, cordially hated by the people, but a favorite both of the King and the Queen.[1] They had given him the highest honors and titles possible in Spain, and finally they had made him a present of the territory of Texas. To this princely gift they added soldiers and ships,

Old Stone Fort at Nacogdoches.

and a large number of young women from the asylums in Spain. Godoy in his dreams already saw himself ruling in a semi-barbaric fashion over his kingdom in the "golden west."

The attitude of Napoleon Bonaparte toward Spain put an end to this curious scheme. Soldiers and ships were ordered to another service; the young women were returned to their asylums; and Godoy was sent into dishonorable exile with his pocket empty, at least of Texas.

[1] Charles IV. and Maria Louisa of Parma.

Spain, tired of the troublesome present she had received from Louis the Fifteenth, one fine day in 1800 handed Louisiana back to France. But before the French colonists had time to rejoice, Napoleon in 1803 sold them and their province to the United States. Again they were very angry; but, as before, nobody cared in the least what they thought or how they felt.

The old dispute concerning the boundary between Louisiana and Texas was revived by this transaction. Spain claimed eastward as far toward the Mississippi River as she dared. The United States would gladly have reached out westward to the Rio Grande. The quarrel at last grew so bitter that both countries prepared to go to war (1806).

Nacogdoches and Natchitoches glared at each other across the Sabine River, like two watch-dogs snarling and showing their teeth.

Antonio Cordero, governor of Texas, hurried by way of the Old San Antonio Road from San Antonio to Nacogdoches. The lonely presidio then fairly thrilled; for fortifications were thrown up, provisions were brought in, and the place was put in a state of defense. Soldiers were also stationed at the mouth of the Trinity River, at the old fort at Adaes, and at other points. At length in August, 1806, Simon Herrera, commanding the Spanish troops with Cordero as his second, marched in with twelve hundred men at his back.

At Natchitoches also there was bustle and excitement. Governor Claiborne, followed at once by General Wilkinson of the United States army, had come up from New Orleans. Several angry messages passed between Generals Wilkinson and Herrera; but neither would yield an inch in his demands; and on the 22d of October General Wilkinson marched his troops to the east bank of the Sabine River and camped there. General Herrera's camp was on the west bank, just opposite. The stream alone separated the two armies. On both sides everything was in readiness for a battle.

But in the hush of the night (November 5) the two generals met and held a secret council. The next day (Nov. 6, 1806), to the surprise of all and greatly to the disappointment of the American soldiers, it was announced that the affair had been peacefully settled. A strip of land between the Sabine River and a creek called the Arroyo Hondo seven miles west of Natchitoches, was declared neutral ground, — that is, ground to be occupied by neither country until the boundary line could be fixed by a state treaty.[1]

The Americans marched away, grumbling openly; the Spanish generals, having got more than they expected, returned well pleased to Nacogdoches.

Nacogdoches had ceased to be simply a stopping-place for travelers; it vied with its distant neighbor, San Antonio, in the gaiety of its social life. The Spanish officers, especially the commandant Herrera, were noted for their gracious and courtly manners. Some American families of position had moved in; there was even a hotel. The presidio had become a town.

3. THE NEUTRAL GROUND.

One day in 1812 a young man — an American — wearing the uniform of the United States army crossed the Arroyo Hondo on horseback and entered the Neutral Ground. He withdrew a little from the road, dismounted, and seated himself upon a fallen log, seeming to await some one or something.

[1] Natchitoches is about forty miles from the Sabine River in a direct line. The Neutral Ground, therefore, was about thirty-three miles wide. It extended southward to the mouth of the Calcasieu River. The choice of the Arroyo Hondo as a boundary was the revival of an old compromise. The French and Spanish commandants, as early as 1719, agreed upon the Arroyo Hondo as a convenient boundary between Louisiana and New Spain. This agreement was observed until 1762, when the whole of Louisiana west of the Mississippi was ceded to Spain. The Sabine River, by a state treaty (1819), was finally fixed as the boundary.

Soon a second rider appeared, threading his way through the forest trees. He was a Spaniard of soldierly bearing, and his somewhat stern features offered a marked contrast to the eager face of the first comer. He dismounted with a courteous greeting, sat down in his turn, and drawing a map from his pocket, he spread it upon his knees.

The Spaniard was Colonel Bernardo Gutierrez de Lara. The American was Lieutenant Augustus Magee.

The Neutral Ground from the moment of the treaty between Herrera and Wilkinson in 1806 became the resort of all sorts of lawless men, who, subject to no authority, robbed and murdered at will the travelers passing across this No Man's

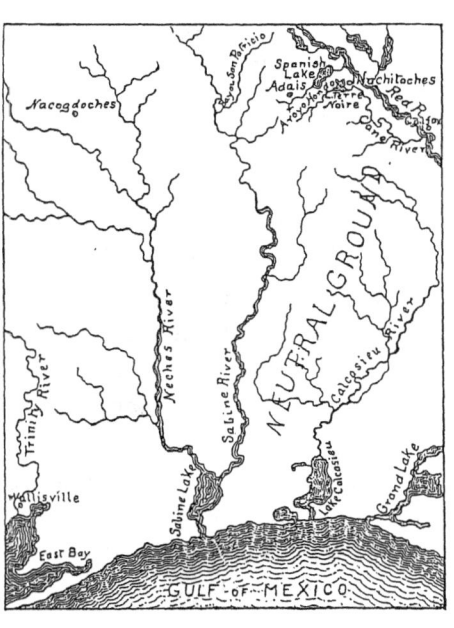

Map of The Neutral Ground.

Land. The danger at last became so great that the United States sent a squad of soldiers to serve as an escort to people whose business led them between the Sabine and Natchitoches. Lieutenant Magee was placed in command of this escort. He was a bold and gallant young fellow, within whose romantic brain soon came the idea of following out Nolan's supposed plan of founding an independent republic in Texas.

He confided his project to Gutierrez, who had fled to Natchitoches after the failure of a similar attempt in Mexico, in which he had taken part. Gutierrez was delighted. He undertook to gain over the Mexicans in Texas. Magee resigned his position in the United States army and soon succeeded in forming a band composed of adventurers and desperadoes from the Neutral Ground, a number of Indians, some Mexicans, and a few Americans of good character. Gutierrez, on account of his influence over his countrymen, was put in command. Magee, however, was the leading spirit.

It was to talk over their scheme of invasion and conquest, to consult maps and arrange routes, that Magee and Gutierrez had met on the banks of the Arroyo Hondo.

Magee started soon after for New Orleans to get money and recruits. Gutierrez with a few men crossed the Sabine and took possession of Nacogdoches, which was at once abandoned by the Spaniards. From that place he marched to join Magee and the main army on the Trinity River.

The first movement of this army of republicans, which numbered several hundred men, was upon La Bahia (Goliad). The Spanish garrison in the fortress there joined them, surrendering, along with other military stores, the cannon brought over by La Salle in 1685.

Hardly, however, were the republicans within the fort when they were attacked by the Spanish army, under Governor Salcedo and General Herrera.

The fighting was at great odds, but the little band of republicans held their own during several months, their greatest loss being the death of their brave and spirited young leader, Magee, who, wasted with consumption, died in February, 1813.

Shortly afterwards a fierce hand-to-hand skirmish took place. In this the republicans were victorious. The Spaniards thereupon gave up the siege and retreated to San Antonio. The republicans followed under Colonel Kemper, who had succeeded Magee. On the 28th of March, 1813, a bloody battle took place on the Rosillo Creek, nine miles from San Antonio. The Spaniards were defeated with the loss of one thousand men. The victorious army marched into San Antonio, flying their flag in triumph. In the fortress of the Alamo they found seventeen prisoners, whom they released; the private soldiers taken prisoners at Rosillo were all set at liberty. The officers were at first paroled; but afterward by order of Gutierrez, or at least with his consent, they were marched by a company of Mexican soldiers to a place on the river below the town; there they were stripped, their hands were bound behind their backs, and their throats cut.

Among those thus brutally butchered were Salcedo, Governor of New Leon, Governor Cordero, and the brave and polished Herrera.

Many of the better class of Americans, among them the commanding officer, Colonel Kemper, disgusted with the savagery of Gutierrez, left the army. The republicans who remained were filled with triumph; intoxicated with success, they gave themselves up to rioting and rejoicing.

Their enthusiasm was increased by a victory over another Spanish force sent against them under the command of Don Y Elisondo (El-ee-son'do). In this battle, fought June 4, the Spaniards lost over a thousand men, dead, wounded, and prisoners.

But the tide of success had reached its height; it began to turn. Gutierrez having retired to Natchitoches, General Toledo (To-lā'do) was now in command of the republicans. On the 18th of August he marched out of San Antonio to attack a third Spanish army commanded by General Arredondo, who had thrown up breastworks on the Medina near the town.

The result was a terrific defeat for the republicans. Almost the entire army was destroyed; many were killed; those taken prisoners were butchered as cruelly as Herrera and his brother officers had been. Out of eight hundred and fifty Americans, only ninety-three escaped. One by one these stole through Nacogdoches on their way back to the safe thickets of the Neutral Ground.

4. THE RED HOUSE.

Nacogdoches, it may be supposed, had grown accustomed to that dream of a Texas Republic which from time to time caused the air about her stone fort to thrill and vibrate; she was accustomed, too, to see that dream end in bloodshed and death.

So it was an old story when in 1819 some three hundred Americans came tramping in, ready, as they imagined, to convert Texas into a free and independent state. This new expedition, organized at Natchez, Mississippi, was conducted by Dr. James Long of Tennessee, an energetic patriot who had served as a surgeon in Jackson's army at the battle of New Orleans.

General Long's brother, David, accompanied him; and his wife and her sister followed, under the conduct of Randall Jones. They arrived at Nacogdoches soon after the new republicans had taken peaceful possession of the town.

A legislative body was formed. One of its members was Bernardo Gutierrez, who had continued to live at Natchitoches. The Republic of Texas was proclaimed, and land and revenue laws were passed. A newspaper, the first in Texas, was started by Horatio Bigelow, a member of the council.

General Long's next step was to take possession of the country and strengthen the infant government. He placed detachments of men at various points on the Brazos and Trinity Rivers, opened trade with the Indians, and sent James Gaines, one of his lieutenants, to Galveston Island to get the assistance of Lafitte.

Jean Lafitte, a Frenchman by birth, had, while yet a mere lad, commanded a privateer which sailed the Gulf of Mexico. Later, with his two brothers, he had been, nominally, a blacksmith in New Orleans; but while hammering horseshoes and making wagon-tires, he was really engaged in smuggling. After a while, he dropped all pretense, and gathering together a band of reckless men he established himself in 1810 on the island of Grand Terre, a swampy lowland in Louisiana near the Gulf coast. From there he plied his unlawful trade. His band became finally so bold and troublesome that a reward was offered for their leader's head. This proclamation, signed by Governor Claiborne, was posted about New Orleans; and more than once the daring freebooter was seen talking gaily with a group of friends, leaning the while with folded arms against a wall upon which flamed in big letters the governor's mandate demanding his head. He was never captured.

In 1814, when the United States and England were at war, a British officer visited Lafitte at Grand Terre and offered him the command of a frigate if he would join the British navy. Lafitte instead offered his services to General Jackson, fought

Jean Lafitte.

gallantly at the battle of New Orleans, and received a full pardon from the United States government.

But his restless spirit would not long suffer him to remain inactive. In 1816 he fitted out a schooner (*The Pride*) and sailed to the uninhabited island of Galveston.

This island was discovered by La Salle as he coasted along the Gulf in 1684, seeking the Mississippi River. He called it the Island of St. Louis. It was afterward known as Snake Island, and received its present name, about 1775, in honor of Don José Galvez, governor of Louisiana and son of the viceroy of Mexico.

It had been occupied for a short time (1816) by a band of Mexican "republicans," under Manuel Herrera and Xavier Mina. They were joined by Luis d'Aury, a Mexican naval officer, and Colonel Perry, an American who had taken part in Magee's ill-fated expedition. They set up a sort of republic on the island. Their fleet of twelve armed vessels sailed the Gulf, and for a time the enterprise prospered. But the little republic did not last long. The leaders quarreled among themselves; the United States denounced their sailors as pirates; the settlement was broken up, and Galveston returned to its native solitude.

The island was covered with beautiful green grass; there were no shrubs, and the only trees were three live oaks clustered together about midway of the island. Its wide beach shone like silver in the sunlight. Here in a short time Lafitte had established a miniature kingdom. Adventurers came flocking to him from every direction, and in less than a year there were a thousand persons on the island. Lafitte, bearing the proud title of "Lord of Galveston," held absolute sway over them. The fort and the town, which he named Campeachy, were kept under strict military rule. The bay harbored a fleet of swift vessels, sailed by fearless pirates who swept the Gulf, capturing and plundering Spanish ships and bringing the rich spoils to be divided by their chief. On the incoming Spanish barques there were bales of silks and satins, woven for the dark-eyed dames of Mexico, and soft carpets and priceless hangings for their houses; there were rare wines for the tables of the viceroys, and gold-embroidered altar-cloths for the churches. On outgoing Mexican vessels there were bars of silver and ingots of gold, tropical spices and dyes, uncut jewels, and beautiful skins of wild animals. All these treasures were unrolled and spread out on the open square of the fort, and each man was allotted his share. Lafitte was generous with the goods brought in by his freebooters. Once from a rich "haul" he took for his own share only a slim gold chain and seal which had been removed from the neck of a portly Mexican bishop on his way to visit Rome. This chain and seal were given by the pirate to Rezin Bowie, a brother of James Bowie. It remains in the Bowie family to this day.

Besides the regular business of piracy, which was politely called privateering, a brisk slave-trade was carried on between the island and the shores of Africa. Slave-ships came boldly into the harbor and landed their cargoes of black humanity at Campeachy. The negro gangs were driven into the fort, where they were sold *by the pound*. The price paid was generally one dollar a pound, though prices sometimes fell so low that an able-bodied man or woman could be bought for forty dollars. The purchasers hurried the unhappy Africans through the country to Baton Rouge and New Orleans, where they were resold at higher prices.

Lafitte was adored by his followers, though he ruled them as with a rod of iron. In person he was tall, dark, and handsome, with stern eyes and a winning smile. He wore a uniform of dark green cloth, a crimson sash, and an otter-skin cap. He lived in great state, in a richly furnished dwelling, called, from its color, the "Red House," and entertained there in an almost princely manner the strangers whom business, curiosity, or misfortune brought to the island.

The Carankawae Indians, who had formerly held the strip of silver sand as their own fishing-ground, visited the new-comers, and gazed with wonder at their ships, their houses, and their cannon. But in a short time a quarrel arose between some of the freebooters and the chiefs, and four of Lafitte's men were killed.

Lafitte hastened to avenge their death. He marched to the Three Trees, where three hundred Carankawaes were encamped. His own force numbered less than two hundred, but they were well armed and provided with two pieces of artillery. The

Indians after three days of hard fighting were defeated, and withdrew to the mainland. This defeat increased their hatred of the whites. But they gave no further trouble to Lafitte.

5. THE CHAMP D'ASILE.

The Lord of Galveston was at the height of his power in March, 1818, when a colony composed of his own countrymen sailed into the bay. They were led by General Lallemand, one of Napoleon Bonaparte's old officers. The empire had fallen, Bonaparte was in exile at St. Helena, and Lallemand, no longer happy or safe in France, decided to form somewhere in the New World a *Champ d'Asile* (Place of Refuge). His choice finally fell upon Texas. He left France in October, 1817, with four hundred men and several women and children. He and his brother officer, General Rigaud (the latter being eighty years old), were received with stately courtesy by Lafitte, who assisted them greatly in their preparations for the journey to the place chosen for their colony.

This was on the banks of the Trinity River, about sixty miles from its mouth. When all was ready the two generals, with one hundred men, traveled thither by land; the others set out by water with a number of small boats carrying provisions, ammunition, etc.

After several days' march the land party reached its destination, where the boats should have arrived before them. The boats were not there. Lallemand and his men were already without food, as they had started with an insufficient supply. They began to suffer the pangs of hunger, filled at the same time with anxiety about the missing boats. While in this condition they found in the woods around a sort of wild lettuce, large quantities of which they boiled and ate. No sooner had they eaten than they were seized with violent and deathlike convulsions. Lallemand, Rigaud, and one of the surgeons had not tasted the poisonous herb. But they were powerless to help, the medicines being on the boats.

Thus they were in despair when a Coushatti Indian, drawn by curiosity, came into the camp. He looked with amazement at the ninety-seven men stretched out and apparently dying on the ground. Lallemand, showing him the fatal herb, explained to him by signs what had happened. The Indian sprang swift as an arrow into the forest, and in a short time reappeared, his arms filled with a feather-like weed. It was the antidote of the poison the men had eaten; he boiled and made a drink of it; and, thanks to his skill and kindness, they all recovered.

Some days later the boats arrived. The voyagers had been unable at first to find the mouth of the river, hence the delay.

The colonists went to work with a will upon their settlement. They built four small forts, — Forts Charles and Henry, Middle Fort, and Fort Palanqua, — mounted eight cannons, and hoisted the French flag. Then they busied themselves with their own houses and fields.

They were very happy, these self-exiled French people. They labored in their fields and gardens by day; at night they sang and danced and made merry, looking forward to long and peaceful lives in their new home.

But the grain was hardly ripe in their fields when word came that Spanish soldiers from San Antonio and Goliad· (La Bahia) were marching upon them to destroy them, or to drive them out of the country. They were not strong enough to resist such a force, so they abandoned their cabins and smiling gardens and returned to Galveston. A violent storm swept over the island a few days after their arrival there. Lafitte lost two brigs, three schooners, and a felucca; the unfortunate colonists lost not only their boats, but all their clothing and supplies.

Lafitte gave them the *San Antonio*, a small ship captured from the Spaniards, and provided them with food and clothes. Some of them sailed to New Orleans in the *San Antonio;* others made their way overland to Nacogdoches; thence to Natchitoches, to Baton Rouge, and at length to New Orleans, whence by the kindness of the citizens they were able to get back to France.

6. A TREACHEROUS SHOT.

It was but a few months after Lafitte had so generously aided Lallemand and his colonists, when James Gaines, sent by General Long, came to the island. Lafitte entertained him royally at the Red House, but declined to join Long's enterprise. He thought a Texas republic could be established only by the help of a large army, whereas General Long had but a handful of soldiers.

When Long received Lafitte's reply he started to the island himself, in the hope of changing this decision. But hearing from his wife that a Spanish force under Colonel Perez was moving upon his outposts, he hurried back to Nacogdoches. He found that place deserted; everybody had fled panic-stricken across the Sabine at the approach of the Spaniards. In the meantime Perez attacked the forts on the Brazos and the Trinity, completely routing the garrisons. David Long was among the killed.

General Long's spirit was unshaken. He joined his brave wife on the east side of the Sabine, and made his way, with her to Bolivar Point, where the few followers left to him were encamped.

Just at this time Lafitte was ordered by the United States government to leave the island; his pirates had begun to meddle with American ships. He felt that resistance would be useless; so he gathered his men together, gave them each a handsome sum of money, and, having set fire to his fort and town, he sailed away in *The Pride*, with sixty of his buccaneers and a choice crew. He cruised for some years off the coast of Yucatan, and died at Sisal in 1826.

It was long believed that he buried fabulous treasures — gold, silver, and jewels — both at Grand Terre and at Galveston, but these treasures have never been found. There is a legend among superstitious people at Grand Terre which declares that several times swarthy, dark-bearded strangers have appeared there and dug in a certain place for the buried treasure. They have succeeded each time in uncovering a great iron chest; but as they were about to lift it out, some one has each time spoken, and at the sound the box instantly disappeared. It can be found and removed, the gossips add, only in the midst of perfect silence.

A prettier story is told of the treasure buried at Galveston. This story goes that on the night before he left the island forever, the pirate chief was heard to murmur, as he paced up and down the hall of the Red House: "I have buried my treasure under the three trees. In the shadow of the three lone trees I have buried my treasure." Two of his men overheard him. They stole away down the beach, with picks and spades, determined to possess themselves of their leader's treasure, which they knew must be priceless. They reached the spot, and in the pale moonlight they found the stake set to mark the hiding place. They shoveled the sand away, breathless and eager with greed. At length they found a long wooden box whose cover they pried open. Within, instead of piles of silver, caskets of jewels, and heaps of golden doubloons, they saw with awe and amazement the pale face and rigid form of the chief's beautiful young wife, who had died the day before. This was the treasure of Lafitte!

General Long watched the ships of Lafitte vanish into the distance; then, determined as ever to carry out his plans, he left his wife and a small guard in the fort at Bolivar Point (July, 1821), and went with fifty-two soldiers to Goliad, which he occupied without opposition. Three days later a troop of Mexican cavalry entered Goliad. Long surrendered and was sent a prisoner of war to Mexico. Eight months afterward he was released; but almost at the moment of his release he was shot and instantly killed by a Mexican soldier.

The guard left at the fort at Bolivar Point soon abandoned it in despair. Mrs. Long refused to go with them; she had promised her husband, she said, to await his return, and she stayed on. Her only companions were her two little children and a negro girl. The days passed drearily; summer died into fall, and fall into winter. The provisions gave out, and the forlorn little group almost perished from hunger. Several times the Carankawaes attacked the fort. The courageous woman loaded the cannon and fired upon the Indians, thus keeping them at bay. In the spring of 1822 she learned from some of Austin's colonists of her husband's tragic death. Then only, having fulfilled her wifely trust, she left the fort.

7. A VOICE IN THE WILDERNESS.

In Nacogdoches there is a wonderful elm, a tree which stood in the primeval forest perhaps before the foot of the white man ever trod its paths. Its leafy branches toss in the wind, green and beautiful against the blue sky. Its old trunk has turned into sap for its own growth the sunshine of more years than any living man can remember.

As a springing sapling it may have greeted Hernando de Soto on his westward march. It may have looked down on La Salle journeying through the forest to his untimely death; and on Tonti of the Iron Hand, seeking tidings of his murdered friend. Don Ramon, lying in its shade, may have watched the slow building of the Mission of Our Lady of Nacogdoches;

and St. Denis, riding by, may have paused to cut switches from its down-drooping branches. Nolan, Herrera, Magee, Long, many a soldier, and many an Indian chief in his war-paint and feathers, — all these the old tree has seen come and go.

A soldier of another sort stood in its shade one day in 1821, and looked upon the small yet motley group of people gathered about him. There were a dozen or more frontiersmen, bronzed and bearded, and armed to the teeth; there were a few Mexican soldiers, a Mexican woman or two with coarse mantillas on their heads, and several wide-eyed Mexican children. The man facing this group held a small book in his hand. He was not armed. His eyes shone with a soft light, and when he spoke his voice was full and sweet.

This was the Rev. Henry Stephenson, a Methodist preacher who had come into the wilderness, not to found a republic nor to set up a free and independent state, but to preach the gospel and to make straight the paths of the Lord.

That day, under the old elm, the first Protestant sermon was preached in Texas. At its close a sweet old hymn, which many a man present had learned at his mother's knee, was begun by the preacher, and one by one, and at first half ashamed, the bearded frontiersmen took up the strain until it floated up and away beyond the clustering leaves of the old tree, and soared into heaven.

Eyes long unused to tears were wet when the hymn was ended; and with softened hearts the singers pressed about the man of God to bid him good-bye. For he was on his way to carry the gospel to the utmost western border of Texas.

Even the gentle Mexican women joined in the cheer which followed him as he entered the lonely forest and passed on out of sight.

IV.

SAN FELIPE DE AUSTIN.

(1820-1835.)

1. AN UNEXPECTED MEETING.

MOSES AUSTIN, a rugged and travel-stained American, was walking slowly across the plaza in San Antonio one day in December, 1820. His head hung on his breast, and his eyes were full of trouble and defeat. Suddenly he heard his name pronounced; he turned to find himself face to face with the Baron de Bastrop, who grasped him warmly by the hand. His eyes brightened with pleasure at this unexpected meeting. "I thought myself a total stranger in San Antonio," he said.

Stephen Fuller Austin.

De Bastrop, whom he had met some years before in the United States, listened with great interest while Austin told the story of his plans and their failure.

He was, he said, a citizen of Missouri, where he had settled when that state was Spanish territory. His object in coming to San Antonio was to obtain permission to establish a colony somewhere in Texas. But on presenting himself to Governor Martinez (Mar-tee'ness), after his long and dangerous journey, he had been coldly received and ordered to quit the province.

He was at that moment on his way to the place where he had left his horses and his negro servant, in order to prepare for departure. "My journey, as you see," he concluded, "has been fruitless."

De Bastrop,[1] a Prussian in the service of Mexico, chanced also to be one of the alcaldes of San Antonio. "Come with me again to the governor," he said, leading the way to the official residence. Here he used his influence to such purpose that in a few days Austin was on his way to Missouri with the assurance that his request would be granted by the general government.

But the homeward journey, made in the dead of winter, proved fatal to him. A sickness, brought on by cold and exposure, so weakened him that he died soon after reaching home. Before his death, however he learned that permission had been given him to settle three hundred families in Texas. He left as a sacred legacy to his son Stephen the duty of carrying out his cherished project.

Stephen Fuller Austin, the great pioneer of Texas colonists, was at that time twenty-eight years of age. He was slender and broad-browed, with features which showed at once the gentleness and the firmness of his character. He had inherited his father's self-reliance and energy — the capital most needed in that almost trackless wilderness henceforth to be his home. He was well educated; his manners were courteous and dignified; he inspired with confidence and respect all who came in touch with him. Such, in part, was the man one day to be known as the Father of Texas.

He was in New Orleans, busied about his father's affairs, when he heard of the arrival at Natchitoches of Don Erasmo Seguin, the commissioner sent from Mexico to meet and confer with Moses Austin. He went to Natchitoches without delay, and there learned of his father's death and the solemn obligation laid upon himself.

[1] Baron de Bastrop had been an officer in the army of Frederic the Great.

He accepted the charge without hesitation, and began at once to perfect his plans.

In July he accompanied Seguin back to San Antonio, traveling by the Old San Antonio Road. Martinez received him kindly, and gave him permission to explore the country and select a place for his colony. He chose the rich lands lying between the Colorado and Brazos Rivers.

A contract was made which allowed 640 acres of land to each colonist; to his wife (if married), 320 acres; and 140 acres to each child; 80 acres were allowed to the master for each slave. The colonists, who must be from Louisiana, were required to furnish certificates of good character, to profess the Roman Catholic religion, and to swear allegiance to Spain. They were to be free from taxation for six years. Austin was commissioned to take charge of the local government.

These writings signed, Austin returned to Louisiana to collect emigrants.

2. UPS AND DOWNS.

It was during the Christmas holidays of 1821 that the first settlers, led by Austin in person, reached the Brazos River and made their camp upon the chosen spot. Their Christmas and New Year's dinners were not composed of dainties, we may be sure; but there was, no doubt, joyous roasting of wild game over the glowing camp-fires, and there was good honest fun and innocent merriment in plenty among these first Texans!

Their leader left them at once and proceeded to Matagorda Bay to meet the *Lively*, a small schooner which had been sent out from New Orleans with supplies for the settlement. She had also carried eighteen colonists.

The *Lively* had not arrived, nor was she ever heard of afterward. It is supposed that she was lost at sea, with all on board. To add to Austin's disappointment, some provisions brought on a former voyage of the *Lively*, and hidden in the canebrakes on the banks of the Brazos, had been stolen by the Carankawae Indians. He returned empty-handed to his people.

They were in no wise cast down by the news he brought. They were already making clearings, cutting down trees, burning underbrush, building cabins, and laying off fields. They were at the same time obliged to keep guard day and night against the Indians who prowled about, always on the lookout for a chance to steal or to murder.

Austin, cheered by their courage, set out for San Antonio to report to Governor Martinez. There he learned that a revolution against Spain had taken place in Mexico. His contracts, in the new order of things, might be worthless. He therefore journeyed on to the city of Mexico, twelve hundred miles distant. Much of the way he traveled with but one companion. The country was full of robbers and cut-throats, and, in order to escape their clutches, the two men disguised themselves as beggars, going on foot, sleeping in the open air, and eating the coarsest food. He found the country in such a tumult that it was over a year before he could get his grant renewed and return to his colony.

Meantime, other settlers had come in, some making their way slowly by land with ox-teams, stopping sometimes for a whole season to raise and harvest a crop of corn, and then moving patiently on. "Children were born in these movers' camps," says one writer, "and the dead were buried by the roadside." Others came in ships from New Orleans and Mobile, and even from the far New England coast. In 1822 the *Revenge* and the *Only Son* came into Galveston harbor and landed at Bolivar Point over a hundred immigrants. They found Mrs. Long in the forlorn little fort where her husband had left her, still waiting and hoping for his return. It was from these pitying and kind-hearted pioneers that the heroic wife learned of the assassination of her husband. In their company she and her children left the place of so much suffering.

The first crop of corn — turned into the virgin soil with wooden ploughs — had been gathered; a little cotton had whitened the patches about the cabin doors, and the spinning-wheels were already busy. The familiar low of home-returning milch-cows was heard at sundown along the winding footpaths. One of the settlers (Randall Jones) had gone to Louisiana, taking with him a negro lad. There he traded the boy for sixty head of cattle, which he drove across the country to the settlement. Another colonist brought out some pigs and a few goats. These domestic animals gave a homelike appearance to the strange land.

The settlement was thriving in spite of hardships. But these hardships were almost without number. There was neither salt, coffee, nor sugar. Meat was to be had only by hunting, and oftentimes deer and buffalo were hard to find and, on account of the Indians, dangerous to follow. True, there were great numbers of wild mustangs.

There were no horses in America before the discovery of Columbus. The Texas mustangs were the product of the cavalry horses brought from Europe to Mexico by Cortez in 1519. They had multiplied, almost unmolested, during the three hundred years they had roamed prairie and forest. These mustangs were always fat, and when nothing better was to be had they made tolerable food.

There were, of course, no stores where anything could be bought; the men went dressed in buckskin; the women in coarse cloth woven by themselves. There was no mail; news from the outer world — from the dear ones left behind in the far-away "states" — came only when a chance traveler arrived with an old newspaper or possibly a letter in his saddle bags. There was neither school nor church.

But in those rude cabins dwelt honesty, high courage, and unbounded hospitality. In business every man's "word was as good as his bond." There were no locks on the doors, robbery being unknown. Everything, even to life itself, was ever at the service of friend and neighbor. The nameless traveler, welcomed without question, shared, as long as he chose to stay, the fireside and table of his host.

Of such stuff were the first Texans.

Austin returned from Mexico in July, 1823. He was welcomed with affectionate joy by his colonists. He was accompanied by his father's friend, the Baron de Bastrop, commissioned by the government to assist him in laying off the town, surveying lands, and issuing titles.

The town was named by Señor de la Garza, who had succeeded Martinez as governor of Texas. He called it San Felipe (Fa-lee′pa) de Austin, in honor at the same time of his own patron saint and of its founder.

Other towns soon sprung up over the province; for grants for other settlements had been sought and obtained from the government. Austin got permission in 1825 to bring out five hundred additional families. Immigrants flocked in, eager to share in this cheap and fruitful paradise. The names *Columbia*, *Brazoria*, *Gonzales*, *Victoria*, *San Augustine*, and other towns and settlements, began to be familiar to the tongue.

Some Irish colonists founded on the Nueces River, near its mouth, a town which they named St. Patrick in remembrance of the patron saint of Ireland. To the Spanish-speaking people of Texas it soon became known as San Patricio, and so it is still called.

A large tract of land was granted to Hayden Edwards, a Kentuckian, in the neighborhood of Nacogdoches, the old gateway of Texas history. But things did not go as smoothly there as in Austin's colony. It was too near the Neutral Ground, which continued to harbor outlaws and adventurers of all kinds.

The land, moreover, was claimed by the Mexicans and others who were already settled upon it. The quarrels between these and the newcomers became in course of time so bitter that the Mexican government, during an absence of Hayden Edwards in the United States, took back his grant and ordered him and his two brothers to leave the country.

Edwards had put all of his private fortune into his venture, and this act of tyranny goaded him and his colonists to fury. Finding vain all their appeals to the governor, they took up arms and declared they would make of Texas an independent republic. They called themselves Fredonians; and banding together, they entrenched themselves in the old stone fort at Nacogdoches. Thence they sent an appeal to Austin's colonists for help. Both Austin's colonists and the Cherokee Indians, upon whom they counted for support, refused to join them. News came that a Mexican army was marching against them; their own fighting force was less than two hundred men. They saw the weakness of their position; and the Fredonian war, as it was called, ended after a skirmish or two, in the surrender of the Fredonians. Edwards and his colonists left Texas, and returned angry and disgusted to Louisiana (1826).

This was a small foretaste of Mexican justice. But troubles far graver than the Fredonian war were at that moment brewing for Texas.

3. ORDERS AND DISORDER.

Until 1824 Texas had been a province of Mexico, with her capital at San Antonio. In that year, however, the general government decreed the union of Texas with Coahuila; and the capital of the new state was fixed at Saltillo (Sal-tee'yo), a distant town in Mexico. A department chief was the only official stationed at San Antonio. The colonists were much displeased at this change. Instead of a ride, when necessary, to San Antonio, where there were friends and familiar faces,

SAN FELIPE DE AUSTIN.

torch-lit plazas, music, and *fiestas* to welcome the traveler, it meant a long and perilous journey through a strange land, among people who regarded all Americans with an eye of sullen distrust.

The Mexicans can hardly be blamed for their lack of confidence. They had just shaken off the yoke of Spain; and they saw the Americans — people of a different race, speaking a different tongue, strong, energetic, and masterful — drawing daily nearer to the Rio Grande River. They saw this alien people settling upon rich and productive lands, but paying no taxes; giving nominal allegiance to the Mexican government, but taking no interest in her political affairs. Added to this uneasiness was a growing hatred of the United States, which wished to annex Texas and had already offered to buy the province. Mexico resolved to crush this rising power.

The Americans, on their side, were restless. They did not desire absolute independence; but they wished for a separate state within the Mexican Republic. They therefore, for political as well as for personal reasons, resented the change of capital.

Still further changes were at hand. Bustamente (Boos-ta-men'tä), a cruel and overbearing man, who became President of Mexico in 1830, on taking his seat issued a set of laws forbidding Americans either to locate in Texas or to trade with her people. In place of colonists from the United States, criminals and disabled soldiers from Mexico were to settle the country. The introduction of slaves was prohibited; taxes were put upon almost everything in daily use; customhouses were established for the collection of these duties; armed troops were quartered in different places at the expense of the colonists; and military rules were enforced.

It is needless to say that these laws were not obeyed. Texas was like a nest of angry hornets whose center of action was at San Felipe; a buzz of indignation filled the air; meetings were everywhere held to protest against the injustice and tyranny of Mexico.

The excitement was increased by the arrest and imprisonment of some Texans (1832) by Colonel Juan Davis Bradburn, an American in command of the Mexican Fort Anahuac (An-ah'wak) on Galveston Bay. Among these were William B. Travis (the future hero of the Alamo) and Patrick Jack. William Jack, a brother of the latter, called a meeting at San Felipe, where it was determined to resort to arms, if necessary, for the release of the prisoners, whose offense was trifling.

The state of feeling was clearly shown by the number of men who declared themselves ready to join in attacking Bradburn in his fort. The affair, however, was settled without bloodshed. Colonel Piedras, the Mexican commandant at Nacogdoches, hastened to Fort Anahuac. There, after an investigation of the case, he released the prisoners and placed Bradburn himself under arrest.

In the meantime a fight had taken place between the Mexican garrison at Fort Velasco, at the mouth of the Brazos River, and one hundred and twelve Texans, who had been aroused by the tyranny of Bradburn. Not one of these Texans had ever before been in a battle; their coolness and bravery under fire gave them the measure of their own power. They were victorious. Colonel Dominic Ugartechea (U-gar-tā-chā'a), the commandant of the fort, whose personal courage won the admiration of the Texans, surrendered, with a loss of thirty-five killed and thirteen wounded. Of the Texans seven were killed and twenty-seven wounded.

These encounters increased the public excitement to frenzy. But the excitement was suddenly allayed by news from Mexico. The patriot Santa Anna had "pronounced" (declared) against Bustamente.

Santa Anna at this time was looked upon in his own country as a patriot; he had been a leader during the war with the

Spanish royalists, and active in deposing Iturbide (Ee-toor-bee′dā) (1822) when that officer had crowned himself Emperor of Mexico. He had always professed great love for the Texas colonists; and now his bold stand against Bustamente gave assurance that the rights of the colonists would thenceforth be respected. The Texans were wild with enthusiasm, and they gladly pledged their support to Santa Anna, the "generous and high-minded patriot."

Santa Anna.

Santa Anna was elected President of Mexico. His disposition towards Texas continued so friendly that it seemed a good time to make an appeal to his government for a separation of the state of Texas from Coahuila.

A convention met at San Felipe in April, 1833. Delegates were present from all the districts. The streets of the little town on the Brazos echoed under the tread of men who were afterwards to write their names in the Republic's book of gold. Sam Houston, the future hero of San Jacinto, was present as a delegate; David G. Burnet, who was to become the first President of the Republic of Texas; Erasmo Seguin; William H. Wharton; Branch T. Archer; and Stephen F. Austin, the Father of Texas.

A constitution was framed, and a memorial was written to the general government, asking for separation from Coahuila and the repeal of Bustamente's odious decrees.

Austin carried these papers to the Mexican congress. His breast swelled with hope as he drew near the city of Mexico and the "high-minded patriot" Santa Anna.

But the Vice-President, Gomez Farias, had no time to listen to so trifling a thing as a memorial from Texas colonists. As for President Santa Anna, he was shut up in his country-house (Manga de Clavo) laying plans for overthrowing the Mexican constitution and making himself dictator.

Sick at heart over his vain attempts to get a hearing from the government, Austin started home. But a letter which he had written to Texas, advising the people to organize a separate state without further appeal to Mexico, had been sent back to Farias as a treasonable document. Austin was arrested at Saltillo, taken back to the city of Mexico, and put in prison, where he remained for nearly two years. A part of that time he was in solitary confinement.

During his imprisonment he kept a diary. He says of himself on one of these loose pencil-written leaves: "In my first exploring trip in Texas, in 1821, I had a very good old man with me, who had been raised on the frontier, and was a very good hunter. We had not been many days in the wilderness before he told me: 'You are too impatient to make a hunter.' Scarce a day passed that he did not say to me: 'You are too impatient — you wish to go too fast.' Before my trip was ended I saw the benefit of his maxim, and I determined to adopt it as a rule in settling the colony which I was then about to commence in Texas. . . . I believe the greatest error I ever committed was in departing from that rule as I did in the city of Mexico in October, 1833. I lost patience at the delays in getting the business of Texas dispatched, and in a moment of impatience wrote an imprudent, and perhaps an intemperate, letter to the council at San Antonio." "How happy," he says in another place, "how happy I could have been on a farm, . . . free from all the cares and difficulties that now surround me. But I thought it was my duty to obey the call of the people and go to Mexico as their agent."

In October, 1834, he was admitted to a conference with

Santa Anna, who promised to "meditate maturely" the repeal of some of Bustamente's laws. He expressed so much love for Texas that Austin wrote to his people in a burst of thankfulness, "All is going well." But he was himself still detained, and it was not until September, 1835, that he was allowed to return to Texas.

The Texans, despite Austin's letter of assurance, knew that all was not going well. They were, in fact, so convinced that all was going ill that they met in the different towns and organized committees of safety for protection against the Indians (who had become very troublesome), and to take charge of all public matters. At a meeting held in San Felipe October 1, 1834, it was openly proposed to make Texas a separate state without the consent of Mexico. But this step was for a time postponed.

The next year the situation was still more gloomy. Santa Anna's congress passed a decree disarming all Texans. General Martin Perfecto de Cos was ordered from Mexico to Texas with a body of five hundred soldiers to enforce the decree, and to punish those who had refused to obey, not the just laws of the Mexican Republic, but the tyrannical edicts of Bustamente and Santa Anna.

At the same time a courier was arrested with dispatches from Ugartechea at San Antonio to the commandant at Anahuac. These dispatches were opened and read at San Felipe. They stated that a strong force would soon reach Anahuac from Mexico.

These things caused great uneasiness and indignation. Another meeting was held in San Felipe. Among those who addressed the people there assembled was R. M. Williamson (called three-legged Willie, because of his carrying a crutch). He counseled resistance. "Our country, our property, our liberty, and our lives," he said, "are all involved in the present contest between the states and the military."

In the midst of the excitement Austin reached home. He was welcomed almost as one given up by the tomb.

It was determined to hold a general consultation to consider the dangers threatening Texas.

The word "consultation" was used instead of "convention" to avoid exciting the jealousy of the government. A convention in Mexico was often followed by a revolution.

A call was issued by Austin for the election of delegates, and the time and place of meeting were fixed for October 16 at San Felipe.

4. A TRUMPET CALL.

A messenger came riding into San Felipe one day; his clothes were dusty, his horse was flecked with foam, his voice was hoarse with excitement. He had ridden hard and fast from Gonzales town, and the news he brought thrilled to the heart's core the men who had gathered about him in the plaza.

Colonel Ugartechea, acting under the decree disarming citizens, had sent an order to Gonzales for a cannon — a four-pounder given by the Mexican government to the townspeople in 1831 for service against the Indians. The order had been peremptorily refused. There were only eighteen men at Gonzales, but they determined to hold the cannon at any cost; and believing that Ugartechea would send an armed force to take it, they had dispatched messengers to the Colorado, the Guadalupe, and the Brazos for help.

The messenger to San Felipe had not finished his story before the men were in their saddles, or girded for the long tramp. They were already armed for the purpose of intercepting General Cos on his march to San Antonio.

When they reached Gonzales they found that the Mexican captain Castenado, had appeared there (September 29) with one hundred cavalrymen and made his demand for the cannon.

He had been put off with the pretext that the alcalde was absent, thus giving the volunteers time to arrive.

The Mexicans had remained on the west bank of the Guadalupe River, the ferryboats having been removed by the Texans to the east or town side on the approach of the enemy

With the recruits from the Brazos, the Colorado, and the Guadalupe, the Texans on the 30th numbered one hundred and sixty fighting men. They then informed Castenado that he could not have the cannon. Moreover, Major Williamson (three-legged Willie) and some others drew the disputed piece of artillery to the river-bank, and placed above it a placard bearing in large letters the challenge, "Come and Take It."

In response to this taunt Castenado made an effort to cross his troops over the river; but the fords were too well guarded, and he finally moved away and encamped a short distance from the river.

R. M. Williamson.

On the evening of the 1st of October the Texans, under the command of Colonels John Moore and J. W. Wallace, crossed the Guadalupe, carrying their four-pounder with them. The same night at eleven o'clock they were formed into a hollow square. Colonels Moore and Wallace, with the Rev. W. P.

Smith, rode into the square, where the minister, being seated on his favorite mule, made them a spirited address. "Fellow soldiers," he said, "the cause for which we are contending is just, honorable, and glorious — our liberty. . . . Let us march silently, obey the commands of our superior officers, and, united as one man, present a bold front to the enemy. *Victory will be ours.*"[1]

On the morning of the 2d they advanced under cover of a heavy fog to a high mound in the prairie where the enemy was posted. After the exchange of a few picket shots a parley took place between Colonel Moore and Captain Castenado. But they could come to no agreement, so they returned to their respective commands. The Texans at once opened fire with their saucy little cannon, and in a short time the enemy was put to rout. The Mexicans retreated toward San Antonio, having lost several men. The Texans, without the loss of a man, returned in triumph to Gonzales with their precious cannon.

This was the first trumpet call to the war of independence. The alarm leaped from town to town. Texas, like a trooper who stands with his foot in the stirrup awaiting but the blast of a bugle, sprang at once into action. There was everywhere an eager note of preparation.

A few days after the victory at Gonzales, Captain George Collingsworth, with about fifty planters from Caney and Matagorda, marched from the latter place to capture Goliad. Just about midnight on the 9th of October, as they approached the town, they were hailed by a man who came out of a mesquit thicket on the roadside. It was Benjamin Milam. He had escaped from prison in Monterey, where he had been placed for opposing the tyranny of Santa Anna, and, worn out by his long journey, he had thrown himself on the ground to rest.

Milam was a man of high courage and stern patriotism. He had taken part — always on the republican side — in several

[1] *Texas Scrap Book.*

of the bloody revolutions in Mexico, and he had been in almost every prison from the Rio Grande to the city of Mexico.[1]

He offered his services to the little band of patriots. They welcomed him with joy into their ranks.

They marched on, and during the night fell upon the unsuspecting garrison at Goliad. The sentinel who fired upon them was killed. The commandant Colonel Sandoval was taken prisoner in his own room, the door of which was broken open with axes. Several officers and twenty-five private soldiers surrendered, the others having escaped in the *mêlée*. The spoils which fell into the hands of the Texans by this exploit were very valuable. They consisted of three hundred stands of arms, several cannon, and about ten thousand dollars worth of military stores.

5. OUT OF A MIST.

San Felipe was not behindhand in enthusiasm over the tidings from Gonzales. Delegates to the General Consultation were coming in, and the committee, on hearing the news, sent out a circular calling upon each man in Texas to decide for himself whether or not he would submit to the tyranny of Mexico, and if he would not submit, "let him answer by mouth of his rifle." This charge was not needed. Men poured in from every quarter carrying their rifles, shot-pouches, and powder-horns; the look of grim determination on their faces meant "liberty, or war to the death."

Austin, by permission of the convention, left San Felipe for

---

[1] Benjamin Milam was a native of Kentucky. He fought in the War of 1812 against Great Britain. In 1823 he received from the Mexican government, for services rendered in the deposition of Iturbide, one million of acres of land in Texas, which he sold to Baring & Co., London.

He also obtained from the government of Coahuila and Texas the exclusive right to run steamboats on the Colorado River. He was unable, however, to avail himself of this right.

Gonzales, arriving there on the 10th of October. He was elected to the command of the volunteers there assembled, about three hundred and fifty strong, and marched almost immediately for San Antonio, hoping to capture and hold that important post. He encamped on the 20th at the Mission of

Mission of La Espada.

La Espada on the San Antonio River. Recruits came in rapidly. Sam Houston, who had given his last five-dollar bill to a messenger to spread the call for volunteers, arrived with a detachment of men from East Texas. Bowie and Travis, Crockett and Fannin, Milam, Burleson, "Deaf" Smith, Rusk, Wharton, — these gathered in groups about the camp, little dreaming that each man of them carried within his own breast something of which the history of Texas was to be made.

General Cos had arrived and had taken command at San Antonio. He scornfully rejected Austin's summons to surrender, even threatening to fire upon his flag of truce. Austin, whose army now numbered about six hundred men, did not feel himself strong enough to make an attack, but decided to move nearer the enemy. Accordingly on the 27th he sent Captains Bowie and Fannin with ninety-two men to reconnoiter and to choose a suitable position. They marched up the river-bank and encamped at nightfall in a bend of the river, near the old Mission of Concepcion.

The next morning at sunrise, through the mist that hung like a grey curtain around the camp, they heard something like the wary tread of horses' hoofs. At the same time a sentinel[1] posted in the high tower of the mission gave warning, and a shot echoed from the outer picket-line.

The Texans sprang to arms; a slight lifting of the fog showed them a solid phalanx of Mexican cavalry hemming in the camp on three sides. There was a breathless interval of preparation, but no confusion; and by the time the enemy's infantry came in sight trailing their arms, the Texans were ready for the fight. It was a short and sharp one.

The encampment had been well chosen; the triangular bottom land in which it lay by the riverside was skirted by heavy timber, and the bluff surrounding it made a sort of natural parapet.

"In a few moments the Mexicans shoved forth their cannon, — a brass six-pounder, — and their bugle sounded a cavalry charge. But one set of gunners after another fell dead or wounded around the cannon, and the cavalry was beaten back. Finally, by a sudden impulse, the whole body of Texans rushed forward with the cry, "The cannon and victory!"

The battle had lasted thirty minutes. The Texan loss was one man (Richard Andrews) killed; none wounded. The Mexicans, whose force numbered four hundred, had sixty killed and about as many wounded. These, in the pell-mell retreat of the attacking party, were left upon the field. About

[1] Robert Calder.

noon a white flag was seen coming across the prairie. It was carried by a priest sent by General Cos, who asked and obtained permission to bury the dead.

The main army, which had marched from La Espada on hearing the cannon, arrived after the battle was over.

Some days later Austin camped with his troops near San Antonio, and prepared to hold his position until strong enough to storm the place.

But inaction, after the brilliant successes at Gonzales, Goliad, and Concepcion, was galling to the volunteers. They clamored to be allowed to throw themselves against Cos' fortifications, and when they were held back many of them grew dissatisfied and left the army. Those who remained were cheered by the arrival of the Grays — two fine companies of volunteers from New Orleans — and a company from Mississippi.

Another incident which revived their drooping spirits was a lively skirmish on the morning of November 26. The approach of a train of mules from Mexico, loaded with silver for General Cos, had been reported by spies to General Edward Burleson, then in command of the army. Colonel Bowie with a small scouting party was on the watch for its appearance.

A scout riding up reported about two hundred Mexican cavalry advancing from the west, guarding a number of loaded pack-mules. Bowie sent the scout on to Burleson for assistance, and dashed forward with his men to cut off the train. On his approach the Mexican cavalry posted themselves in a ravine about one mile from San Antonio. Bowie charged them, but at that moment he was attacked in the rear by a body of Mexican soldiers, who, seeing the situation, had come out from San Antonio, bringing two cannon with them. Bowie wheeled and rode upon this new force, and Burleson coming up with reinforcements, the Mexicans were put to flight, abandoning pack-mules and packs, and leaving on the field fifty men killed and several wounded.

When the Texans, who had come off without a scratch, threw themselves upon the bulky packs ready to count out Mexican dollars, they found them filled, instead, with fresh grass cut for the feed of General Cos' horses. This skirmish was known as the Grass Fight.

6. THE PRIEST'S HOUSE.

While these things were happening at San Antonio, the General Consultation was in session at San Felipe. General Austin, appointed special commissioner to the United States, had resigned his position as commander-in-chief of the army two days before the Grass Fight.

Edward Burleson, who succeeded to the command, had fought under General Jackson in the Creek war, and was known throughout Texas as a brave and intrepid Indian fighter. To him the soldiers now looked confidently for immediate action; and all eyes were turned eagerly toward the citadel over which floated the Mexican flag.

The old town beloved of St. Denis still hugged the river-bank, buried in evergreen foliage and gay with ever-blooming flowers. The stone and adobe houses, with flat roofs, thick walls, and barred windows, lined the narrow streets which opened out into the Military Plaza and the old *Plaza de las Islas* (now Constitution). These plazas had been fortified, and the streets leading into them were barricaded and guarded by cannon. On the east side of the river the fortress of the Church of the Alamo and its walled enclosure had also been fortified and mounted with artillery.

General Burleson, aware of these fortifications, looked at the citadel and at his little army, and, courageous though he was, he stopped to count the cost. While he was hesitating and his men were openly fretting, three Americans escaped from San Antonio, where they had been imprisoned, and came into the camp (December 3). Their report of the enemy's condition decided Burleson to attack the place at once. The order was given and a plan of assault arranged. The soldiers were jubilant; an activity long unknown pervaded the camp. But into the midst of this cheerful excitement dropped like a bombshell a second order countermanding the first. A scout had disappeared, and it was believed that he had deserted in order to warn Cos of the intended attack.

Edward Burleson.

This reason did not satisfy the soldiers. They were defiant and angry almost to mutiny. Their indignation knew no bounds when they were told that the camp was about to be broken and the siege raised. There was a loud clamor of rage and disappointment. During this scene the missing scout returned in company with a deserter from San Antonio, who confirmed the report of the weakness of the defenses and the discontent of the Mexican garrison. Benjamin Milam, upon this, had a word or two with General Burleson in his tent; then he stepped out, bared his head, and, waving his hat with a loud hurrah, demanded in a ringing voice: "Who will go with old Ben Milam into San Antonio?"

Three hundred volunteers with an answering shout sprang to the front.

The same night (December 4) by twos and threes, singly, and in squads, the storming party stole silently into an old mill on the road between the camp and the town. Milam, the chief in command, told them off into two divisions: one to be led by himself and the other by Colonel Frank W. Johnson. Silent still and like phantoms, the double line took up its march over the intervening ground and slipped into San Antonio.

A little earlier, Colonel Neill had started from camp with a detachment to make a pretended attack on the fortress of the Alamo. He opened fire before daylight and continued to hold the enemy's attention until the assaulting party could enter the town. When the sound of their guns apprised him that this was done, he returned to the camp, where General Burleson kept his men under arms, ready to march at any moment to Milam's assistance.

Milam and Johnson, guided by Deaf Smith, drew their men swiftly through the dark and silent streets. Suddenly a sentinel gave the alarm. A shot from Deaf Smith's rifle silenced him forever; and the Texans dashed to cover. The Mexicans poured out of their quarters and attacked them furiously in the houses of Señors de la Garza and Veramendi, where they had taken shelter. They returned the fire with their accustomed coolness, picking off their assailants with unerring aim through loop-holes cut in the thick walls, or from the flat parapeted roofs.

For the next five days the Texans were engaged in fighting and burrowing their way steadily toward the Military Plaza. With cannon booming and scattering grape and canister among them, and the rattle of small arms in their ears, they dug trenches along the streets from corner to corner; they battered down doors; with crowbars and axes they pried openings in walls — fighting the while, now at long range, now in deadly hand-to-hand encounters, and always with defiant smiles on their powder-blackened faces. The weather was wet and cold; the dismal streets were slippery with blood and choked with the débris of battle. Above, in the smoky air flapped from the church tower a black flag which meant "No quarter."

On the third day Milam, leaping from a trench to the entrance of the Veramendi courtyard, was killed. A volley of shot spattered holes in the heavy, green, batten door beside him as he fell. The brave chieftain was buried on the spot consecrated by his own blood. Colonel Johnson was elected leader in his place, and the fighting and burrowing went on. About noon the same day Henry Karnes stormed alone the only house between de la Garza's and the plaza, and forced an entrance with a crowbar under a heavy fire from the enemy.

Henry Karnes, the hero of this exploit, was a trapper from the frontier of Arkansas. He had a genuine love of Indian warfare for its own sake, and in search of it came to Texas with the earliest pioneers. When the trumpet call for volunteers was sounded, he enlisted and soon came to be known, with his celebrated friend and companion Deaf Smith, as one of the best scouts and spies in the army. He had many adventures among the Indians. At one time in single combat with an Apache chief he was wounded and taken prisoner. His fiery red hair, which the Indians supposed to be painted, caused him to be regarded by them as a great medicine man. After his capture they concluded to deprive him of this charm, and, taking him to the nearest stream, they ducked his head under the water to wash the red from his hair. When they found, after nearly drowning him, that the red would not come off, they released him, satisfied that he was a favorite of the Great Spirit. He held the house he had taken, against the enraged Mexicans, until Captain York's company joined him and fortified the position.

"These dogs of Texans are hard to beat off," thought General Cos, listening to the crack of their rifles. His crafty face lightened for one moment, for Ugartechea came in from the Rio Grande, and entered the fortress, in spite of the cordon of guards, with five hundred recruits. But such recruits! Cos' face darkened again. They were five hundred convicts chained together two and two, and driven like sheep by their guards.

SAN FELIPE DE AUSTIN.

On the night of the 8th of December the Texans, by a sudden rush and under a hail of hostile bullets, made themselves masters of the Priest's House. The Priest's House was a large, thick-walled building, commanding the Military Plaza on the north side. The captors at once barricaded the doors and cut loop-holes in the massive walls. A loud cheer carried the news of their success to their comrades outside. "To-morrow!" they shouted joyously.

But the capture of the Priest's House completely demoralized the Mexicans. On the morning of the 9th the cannon at the Alamo ceased their thunder; the black flag was hauled down from San Fernando's tower and a white one went up in its place.

General Burleson entered the city the same day and arranged with General Cos the terms of surrender.[1] By these a large quantity of valuable stores, ammunition, artillery, small arms, and clothing remained in the hands of the victors. The Mexicans to the number of thirteen hundred, after taking an oath not to fight against Texas, were permitted to leave, the officers retaining their arms and private property.

The Texan loss in this five days' fight was two killed and twenty-six wounded; the enemy lost about one hundred and fifty.

General Burleson placed a small garrison in the fortress of the Alamo. The camp was raised, and many of the Texan volunteers scattered to their own homes and firesides, rejoicing in the fact that not a Mexican soldier remained to tread the soil of Texas.

[1] General Burleson had remained in camp during the storming of the city. He entered on the 9th. (Official Report.)

7. BY THE BRAZOS.

In November, just before the fight at Concepcion, Houston, Wharton, and other delegates left Austin's army to take their seats as members of the General Consultation at San Felipe.

Branch T. Archer was elected President of the Consultation.

Many of the members were in favor of an outright declaration of independence ; but the more prudent advised against a step so decisive. A temporary government was therefore agreed upon, and a declaration of adherence to the Republican constitution of Mexico of 1824 was signed and sent out. This declaration also gave the reasons of the colonists for taking up arms against military despotism, and stated that "they would not cease to carry on war as long as Mexican troops were within the limits of Texas."

The convention then elected Henry Smith governor, and James W. Robinson lieutenant-governor of the provisional government. Branch T. Archer, William H. Wharton, and Stephen F. Austin were appointed commissioners to the United States. Houston was made commander-in-chief of the Texan army "to be raised."

Sam Houston, placed in so responsible a place by the Consultation, was born in Virginia, but removed when a child to Tennessee with his widowed mother. He had a strong imperious and wayward disposition which showed itself from his early boyhood. At the age of fourteen he left home and joined a band of Cherokee Indians, was adopted into their tribe, learned their language, and wore their costume. In 1813 he served under Jackson in the Creek war ; and at the battle of Topo-heka,[1] he was struck in the thigh by an Indian arrow ; the barbed head buried itself deep in the flesh. He ordered the man by his side to pull out the arrow. After two vain

---
[1] Horseshoe Bend.

attempts the man, who was the lieutenant of his company, turned away. Houston drew his sword and commanded him again to draw out the arrow. "If you fail," he declared, "I will kill you on the spot." The arrow on the third tug came out, leaving a gaping wound. At this battle he received also two bullets in his shoulder.

He became in rapid turn major-general of the Tennessee militia, member of congress, and governor of his state. While he was governor, and in the full splendor of his brilliant career, he resigned his office in consequence of some private and domestic trouble, which has ever remained a secret, and took refuge among his old friends, the Cherokees, with whom he dwelt for years, living the life of an Indian warrior.

Sam Houston.

In 1832 he went to Washington, D. C., in the interests of the Cherokees, and while there was appointed special Indian agent for the southwest. The same year he visited Texas. At San Felipe he met James Bowie and went with him to San Antonio to treat with the Comanches. In 1833 he settled in San Augustine, whence he went as a delegate to the Consultation of 1835.

Governor Smith and his council continued in session at San Felipe. They provided for the raising and equipment of an army of twelve hundred soldiers, and made arrangements for a small navy.

In December Major William Ward of Georgia arrived at San Felipe. He was in command of three hundred newly enlisted volunteers, known as the Georgia Battalion. He obtained from Governor Smith commissions for his officers and returned to Velasco where he had left his troops. Thence they marched to Goliad. About the same time Colonel Wyatt, with two companies of recruits, came from Alabama; and a little later the Red Rovers, a company from Courtland, Alabama, landed at Matagorda. Doctor Shackleford, the captain, sent a messenger to the governor to say that the Red Rovers placed themselves at the service of Texas to remain, not for a term of three, six, or twelve months, but as long as a man was left of the company, or there was an enemy to be found on Texas soil. This offer was accepted by the governor with gratitude, and the Red Rovers, as well as Colonel Wyatt's volunteers, were ordered to report to Colonel Fannin at Goliad.

Bitter quarrels, however, soon arose between Governor Smith and his council and almost put a stop to all public business. Governor Smith was deposed, and Lieutenant-Governor Robinson was placed at the head of affairs. Finally, after providing for an election for delegates to a convention to be held at Washington on the Brazos March 1, the council adjourned.

About the last of March the following year (1836), the Texans, to keep San Felipe from falling into the hands of Santa Anna, set fire to it themselves. The flames spread from cabin to cabin, roaring around the hearthstones so long noted for their hospitality. They swept past the one-room building where the conventions had been held and devoured the rude, unchinked log-hut in the black-jack grove beyond, where Henry Stephenson had preached, and where the first Sunday School had been organized; they consumed roof-tree and picket and garden-fence, so that in a few hours a heap of blackened ashes alone remained of the cradle of Texas.

V.

GOLIAD.

(1835-1836.)

1. MESSENGERS OF DISTRESS.

ON the 20th of December, 1835, there was a spirited meeting of citizens and soldiers at the old town of La Bahia (Goliad) on the San Antonio River.

La Bahia — which means "the bay" — was already old when Austin laid off his town on the Brazos. Captain Alonzo de Leon, on his way to attack La Salle at Fort St. Louis in 1689, stopped there; and in 1718 Don Domingo Ramon with his troopers and friars built there the Mission of Espiritu Santo (The Holy Ghost) for the benefit of the fierce Carañkawae Indians.

The town had seen stirring times during the century and a half of its existence. There had been many Indian fights in and around the mission church, when the garrison was weak and the priests could not control their red-skinned converts ; it was in the same church in 1812 that Magee's army was besieged, and from its doors his Republicans sallied forth to their victorious hand-to-hand conflict with the Spaniards. Here, too, in 1819, General Long surrendered to the Mexicans and was carried away to a treacherous death.

And here in October, 1835, the Mexican commandant Sandoval had been surprised in his sleep by the Texans, his soldiers made prisoners, and the fort and its stores handed over to his captors.

The General Consultation at San Felipe in November, 1835, had thought it more prudent to declare their adherence to the Mexican republican constitution than to issue a declaration of independence.

The citizens and soldiers of Goliad, on the 20th of December following, boldly set their names to a document resolving "that the former state and department of Texas is and ought to be *a free, sovereign, and independent state.*"

Among the signers were several boys fifteen and sixteen years of age.

This paper was sent to the governor and his council at San Felipe by whom it was disapproved and suppressed. They thought it premature. But it was a straw that showed which way the revolutionary wind was blowing.

Captain Philip Dimitt, who was at the head of this movement, was commandant at the fortress at Goliad with about eighty men under his command.

Over at San Antonio at this time, there was much dissatisfaction among the volunteers remaining there. They were more restless than ever, with their own flag waving above the Alamo and no enemy in sight. They had left their homes and firesides for a purpose. It was fighting they were eager for, not idling around a camp-fire.

They were, therefore, delighted when an expedition was set on foot for the capture of Matamoras on the Rio Grande River. General Houston, who had fixed his headquarters at Washington on the Brazos, wished to place Colonel James Bowie in command of this expedition; but in the confusion arising from the quarrels between Governor Smith and his council at San Felipe, an English physician, named Grant, assumed the leadership (January, 1836).

Dr. Grant had taken part in the storming of San Antonio; he was brave and gallant, and a favorite with his fellow-soldiers. Two hundred volunteers gathered under his standard;

he helped himself without leave to arms and ammunition from the fortress stores, took clothing and provisions from the townspeople, and started for Matamoras.

He halted at Goliad. But only long enough to seize and press into service Captain Dimitt's drove of army horses.

Here by order of the council, who had decided to sustain Grant, he was joined by Colonel Frank W. Johnson, and they marched away, leaving Captain Dimitt indignant and angry.

The citizens and soldiers at San Antonio were likewise indignant and angry; and with far better reason. Colonel Neill, left by Johnson in command of the Alamo with only sixty men, sent to General Houston a report describing the helpless and suffering condition of that place after the high-handed raid of Grant and his volunteers.

Houston was much disturbed by this report. He enclosed it to Governor Smith, requesting him to refer it to the council. The commander-in-chief denounced the action of Grant in strong terms and added:

James Bowie.

"Within thirty hours I shall set out for the army, and repair there with all possible dispatch. I pray that a confidential dispatch may meet me at Goliad. . . . No language can express my anguish of soul. Oh! save my poor country! Send supplies to the sick and the hungry, for God's sake!"

He left Washington on the Brazos River on the 8th of January and reached Goliad on the 16th. On his arrival he sent for Colonel Bowie.

James Bowie had come to Texas with Long's expedition.

He was a famous Indian fighter. In 1831, near the old San Saba Mission, with ten companions, including his brother, Rezin Bowie, he had fought one hundred and sixty Comanches and Caddoes, armed with bows and arrows, and guns. The savages surprised and surrounded the little party, discharging their arrows and firing their guns in true Indian fashion from behind rocks, trees, and bushes. The fire was returned, and at every crack of a rifle a redskin bit the dust. The crafty warriors, finding they could not dislodge the hunters, set fire to the dry prairie grass; then they renewed the attack, rending the air with shrill yells. "The sparks flew so thick," said Rezin Bowie afterward, "that we could not open our powder-horns without danger of being blown up." But they held their ground. The Indians drew off at nightfall, and all night long the hunters heard them wailing their dead. The next morning the red warriors had disappeared. Bowie lost but one man in this fight; the Indians had eighty-two killed and wounded.

Bowie was as noted for his coolness and prudence as for his unflinching courage. In person he was tall and fair, with soft blue eyes, and a somewhat careless address. He had married a Mexican lady — the daughter of Vice-Governor Veramendi of San Antonio — and was devoted to the interests of Texas. He was the inventor of the deadly knife which bears his name.

The result of the interview between Houston and Bowie was that Bowie left Goliad the next morning for San Antonio, with a company of thirty men. He bore orders from Houston to Colonel Neill to leave San Antonio, blow up the fort, and bring off the artillery.

Colonel Neill found it impossible to get teams to transport the artillery; he therefore did not carry out any of these instructions. Bowie remained at San Antonio.

Houston made an effort to concentrate at Goliad and Refugio the slender force which made up his army. But he was so hampered by the intrigues and wrangling of the government officials, that early in February he gave up the command and returned to Washington on the Brazos, leaving Colonel James W. Fannin in command of Goliad, with four hundred men.

On the 25th of the same month a messenger came into Goliad. His face was worn with an anxiety which he did not try to conceal ; his eyes were heavy with fatigue. He sought Fannin and had a brief but earnest talk with him. Then he turned, setting his face in the direction whence he had come, and went his way.

This messenger was the fearless and courtly South Carolinian, James B. Bonham. His message was from Colonel Travis, pent up in the fortress of the Alamo and besieged by the army of Santa Anna. He appealed for help from Fannin and the army at Goliad.

On the 28th Fannin started with reinforcements of men and artillery to the relief of Travis ; but before he was fairly on the way his wagons broke down. While he was trying to get them repaired, and at the same time uncertain as to whether he should go on to San Antonio or not, Placido Benevidas (Bā-nā-vee'das), one of Grant's men, came up with weighty news. The Mexican General Urrea (Ur-rā'a) was marching upon Goliad with an army of one thousand men. Fannin returned in haste to the town and began to strengthen his fortifications.

San Patricio, where Grant and Johnson were encamped, was surprised on the night of the 28th of February by Urrea's soldiers. The volunteers, with the exception of Johnson himself and four of his companions who managed to escape, were all captured or killed. Grant, who was out with a squad of men collecting horses, was killed some days later and his body frightfully mutilated.

2. IN CHURCH AND FORTRESS.

A line of blood and flame seemed indeed to be closing upon Texas. General Urrea, after destroying Grant and his volunteers, was advancing toward Goliad with one thousand men. Santa Anna, with an army of seven thousand, had invested San Antonio.

The defeat of General Cos had filled the haughty dictator of Mexico with fury. It was past belief that a handful of the

despised colonists, armed with hunting-rifles, should have put to rout his own well-equipped regulars. He determined to punish this insolence as it deserved. And not only to punish, but to set an iron heel upon the rebellious province.

All prisoners were to be shot; all who had taken part in the revolution were to be driven out of the country; the best lands were to be divided among the Mexican soldiers. The expenses of the rebellion were to be paid by the Texans. All foreigners giving aid to the rebels were to be treated as pirates.

By the 1st of February Santa Anna had sent General Urrea to Matamoras, a town near the mouth of the Rio Grande

River, with orders to proceed from that place against Refugio and Goliad. He himself took command of the main army, with General Filisola (Fee-lee-so'la) as second in command. General Cos and his men, who had taken oath not to bear arms again during the war, joined the army at the crossing of the Rio Grande River. On the 23d of February the first division of this united force appeared on the heights of the Alazan, west of San Antonio.

The soldiers of the garrison were scattered about the town. No warning of a near approach of the enemy had come, and things looked tranquil enough that morning, with the soft winter sunshine flooding the yellow adobe walls and glinting the limpid river.

A cry from the sentinel posted on the roof of San Fernando Church startled the stillness; its echoes leaped from street to street; the alarum bells burst into a clanging peal. The Mexicans were already pouring down the slopes west of the San Pedro River.

The garrison hastily crossed the San Antonio River and entered the fortress of the Alamo. One of the officers, Lieutenant Dickinson, galloped in on horseback, with his baby on his arm and his wife behind him. Some beef-cattle grazing around the fort were driven in and the gates were closed.

Colonel William B. Travis had succeeded Neill in the command of the fort, which was garrisoned by one hundred and forty-five men. Travis was but twenty-eight years of age; confident, bold, determined, and full of patriotic ardor. Colonel James Bowie was second in command.

Among other defenders of the Alamo were Colonel James B. Bonham of South Carolina and David Crockett of Tennessee —" Davy" Crockett, the backwoodsman, bear-hunter, wit, and politician. Crockett had reached San Antonio just before the siege, with a small company of Tennesseeans, and offered his services to Travis. He was a picturesque figure in his fringed and belted buck-skin blouse and coon-skin cap. His long rifle, Betsy, had "spoken" in the war of 1812, and echoed since on many an Indian trail. Its last word was to be spoken at the defense of the Alamo.

The Mission of the Alamo, established in 1703 and several times removed, was finally built, in 1744, on the spot where it now stands. Like the other missions, it was both a church and a fortress. It is on the east side of the San Antonio River, facing the town to westward. The cross-shaped church, slit with narrow windows and partly roofless, stood on the southeast corner of a walled plaza several acres in extent. The other buildings — convent, hospital, barracks, and prison — were within the enclosure. There was also a small convent-yard adjoining the chapel. All of the buildings were of stone; the enclosing walls were built of adobe bricks. The sacristy of the church was used as a powder magazine. The place was defended by fourteen pieces of artillery.

David Crockett.

Santa Anna arrived in person on the 23d. He took possession of San Antonio town and sent a summons to the rebels in the Alamo for unconditional surrender. Travis received and dismissed the messengers with courtesy; then answered by the mouth of a cannon, "No." At the defiant boom which stirred the peaceful air of the valley, a blood-red flag was placed upon the tower of San Fernando, proclaiming "no quarter"; and a thunder of guns opened the attack.

GOLIAD.

The besiegers at first made little headway. If they ventured across the river they were within reach of those unerring rifles they had such cause to dread. It was the third day before they succeeded in planting a battery between the fort and the bridge.

The besieged within the fortress were calm and confident, though they were kept day and night at rifle and cannon. But they were fighting at fearful odds. Travis sent out an impassioned appeal to the council for aid. He also dispatched Colonel Bonham to Goliad, asking for Fannin's assistance. At the same time he proudly wrote : " I shall never surrender or retreat."

On the eighth day of the siege thirty-two volunteers from Gonzales succeeded in passing the Mexican lines and entered the fort. Two days later Colonel Bonham slipped in alone, but bringing news that Fannin would march at once with men and artillery. On the 1st of March Travis wrote to the council; it was his last letter. " I shall continue to hold this place," he said, " until I get relief from my countrymen, or I shall perish in the attempt."

But steady as was his spirit, he could not shut his eyes to the fact that the desperate game was well-nigh played out. On the 4th of March he called his men together and made them a short but ringing speech. There was, he told them, no longer any hope of reinforcements; death was staring them all in the face, and nothing remained but to sell their lives as dearly as possible. " Now," he concluded, drawing a line on the ground with his sword, " whoever is willing to die like a hero, let him cross this line." There was not a moment of hesitation. Gravely and silently, one by one, the men, with one exception,[1] stepped across the line and ranged themselves beside their leader. Bowie, who was sick, had himself lifted over in his cot.

[1] A man named Rose, who escaped by leaping from the wall.

Sunday morning, March 6, between midnight and dawn, the final assault was made by the besiegers. The Mexican bugles sounded the notes of *Duquelo* (no quarter); the thunder of cannon followed. The devoted little band of Texans, weary and worn with constant watching and incessant fighting, sprang to arms as cheerfully and quickly as to a holiday parade.

The Mexicans, two thousand five hundred strong, closed about the walls. They were provided with scaling ladders, axes, and crowbars. A cordon of cavalry was placed around the fort to prevent escape.

The enemy advanced in the gray dawnlight, under a deadly fire from the fort. Twice they placed their ladders against the walls, and twice they recoiled before the terrible hail of shot and shell poured upon them from the fort. The third time, driven by their officers at the point of the sword, the soldiers climbed the walls and swarmed over into the enclosure. Then began a stubborn and bloody combat, which strewed the plaza with corpses. The Texans fought grimly, silently, furiously, with pistols, with knives, with the butts of their rifles, dropping one by one, but sending as they fell scores of Mexicans to a bloody death.

It was in the old church, dedicated to peace and prayer, that the last conflict took place. Here Crockett was killed, with Betsey, his long rifle, whose voice had resounded clearly above the uproar, in his hand. Bowie was slaughtered in his cot, after killing several of his assailants. Major T. C. Evans was shot in the act of putting fire to the powder magazine, as he had promised to do in case things came to the worst.

Mrs. Dickinson and her child, with two Mexican women, were in a small arched room to the right of the chapel door. They were saved by the kindness of the Mexican officer, Colonel Almonte.

The tall form of Travis had towered for an instant only above the battle-waves near a breach in the north wall; then he had gone down, his brave heart stilled forever. With his last breath he cried in a voice which rang above the deadly tumult: "*No rendirse muchachos!*" (Don't surrender, boys!)

Bonham fell near him and almost at the same moment.

Before nine o'clock the butchery was complete. Two thousand five hundred Mexicans, cavalry, artillery, and infantry, fresh and unwearied, had conquered after eleven days' siege a handful of poorly armed, outworn "rebels."

Santa Anna directed the assault from a battery near the river. After the carnage was ended he came into the fort. He surveyed the bloody scene with a smile of satisfaction. His victory had cost him a thousand or more of dead and many wounded; but what did that matter? Not a Texan was left to tell the tale of the Alamo!

The next day the dead bodies of the Texans were collected in heaps and burned. The smoke of that fire ascended to high heaven like a prayer for vengeance. The answer when it came was terrible.

Mrs. Dickinson and her child, two Mexican women, and a negro servant belonging to Travis were the only survivors of this massacre. Mrs. Dickinson was placed on a horse with her child in her arms and sent by Santa Anna to the colonists with an insolent message announcing the fall of the Alamo.

3. FORT DEFIANCE.

On the 1st of March the General Convention met at Washington on the Brazos. On the 2d, while Travis' signal guns were still sending their sturdy boom across the prairies, a declaration of independence was read and adopted.

Houston was made commander-in-chief of the armies of the Republic of Texas. David G. Burnet was elected President and Lorenzo D. Zavala Vice-President. Thomas J. Rusk was made Secretary of War.

Sunday, the 6th of March, the day the Alamo fell, Travis' last appeal reached Washington — after the hand that wrote it was cold in death. His letter was read by the President to the members of the convention; it produced a powerful effect. In the first burst of feeling it was even proposed that the convention should adjourn, arm, and march to San Antonio.

Houston spoke earnestly against such a step, and as soon as

Mission at Goliad.

quiet was restored, he himself with two or three companions left for Gonzales, where the new volunteers were ordered to gather.

The air as he rode westward was thick with rumors. He arrived at Gonzales on the 11th. The same day came the first tidings of the fall of the Alamo. It filled the town with a wail of desolation. Of the thirty-two men who had marched from Gonzales to the relief of Travis, and to their own death, twenty had left wives and children behind them.

The arrival of Mrs. Dickinson with her child, and her story of the siege with all its ghastly details, added to the gloom. The moans of the widow and the fatherless mingled with the dreary bustle of preparation for flight. For it was rumored that the bloodthirsty Mexicans were approaching.

General Houston had found three hundred recruits at Gonzales. But they were unprepared for an attack ; they had neither provisions nor munitions of war ; the place was without defenses of any kind. He therefore gave orders for retreat. At nightfall on the 13th the forlorn handful of women and children mounted horses, or clambered into wagons where a few household goods had been hastily piled ; the troops formed around them, and at midnight the march began.

As they moved away across the prairie a light reddened the sky behind them. It came from the flames of their own burning houses. A cry burst from the women, and the eyes already swollen with weeping overflowed again at the sight of their desolated hearthstones.

When Colonel Fannin found himself unable to march to the relief of the Alamo, he reëntered Goliad. He now knew that Urrea was advancing rapidly, and he made haste to strengthen his position. He had at this time five hundred men under his command. They occupied the Mission of Espiritu Santo, called by Fannin Fort Defiance. Earthworks had been thrown up around the old church, ditches dug, and cannon mounted. But the defenses were weak, the men were poorly fed and scantily clad. They were often compelled to mount guard barefoot. Fannin was filled with gloomy forebodings, although the signal-guns of the Alamo, which were to be fired as long as the flag continued to wave over that fortress, were not yet silenced.

About the 12th of March Captain King was sent by Fannin with a small detachment of men to bring away the women and children from Refugio, a small town about twenty miles distant. King was attacked by the advance guard of Urrea's army, and had barely time to throw himself into the mission church at Refugio. From there he sent to Fannin for more troops. Colonel Ward, with one hundred and twenty-five men, immediately joined him in the church where he was entrenched.

The next morning (14th) Captain King with his men left the fort on a scouting expedition. About three miles from the mission they were surprised by a large body of Mexicans, to whom they surrendered. A few hours later they were stripped of their clothing by their captors and shot. Their unburied bodies were left to decay on the open prairie.

The same morning, about ten o'clock, fifteen of Ward's men were sent from the mission to the river about a hundred yards away to get water. They had filled two barrels and placed them on a cart drawn by a couple of oxen, and were about returning to the fort when some bullets sang over their heads. A glance showed them the Mexican army on the other side of the river, not half a mile distant. They hurried on as fast as they could, and reached the mission in safety with a good part of the water. One barrel was emptied of about half of its contents through a hole made by a shot from the advancing enemy.

Urrea attacked the barricaded church. The battle lasted nearly all day, but late in the afternoon he drew off his beaten and discouraged force; he had two hundred killed and wounded. Ward's loss was three wounded.

But the ammunition of the besieged was nearly exhausted, and that night, after supplying the three wounded men with water, Colonel Ward and his men stole quietly out of the church and slipped unseen past the Mexican sentinels.

On the 21st, after weary marches through swamp and thicket and constant skirmishes with the enemy, they surrendered on honorable terms to Urrea, and were taken back to Goliad.

4. PALM SUNDAY.

Fannin turned away from General Houston's messenger on the morning of the 13th (March) with an anxious and gloomy face. The messenger, Captain Desauque, had just come in from Gonzales, leaving woe and despair behind him. He brought the black tidings of the fall of the Alamo, and he bore orders from the commander-in-chief for Fannin to blow up the fort, bury or throw into the river such of the cannon as he could not bring away, and retreat to Victoria on the Guadalupe River.

There was scant time in which to mourn the fall of the Alamo, but the dark looks on the men's faces, as they buried the guns and demolished the fortifications, told of what they were thinking.

Fannin sent a courier to Ward and King, ordering them to return at once from Refugio ; this courier, as well as others sent later, was captured by Mexican scouts.

Fannin waited five days in great suspense, loth to abandon these officers and the women and children whom they had been sent to protect.

At length came the news of Ward's retreat from Refugio. The remaining works of Fort Defiance were destroyed, the buildings were set on fire, artillery and ammunition were loaded on wagons ; the drums called the men from their ruined quarters. Mrs. Cash, the only woman left in Goliad, was placed in their midst, and, with a last glance at Fort Defiance, Fannin began his fatal retreat.

This was on the 19th of March.

The wagons, enveloped in fog, creaked their way across the San Antonio River and over the prairie beyond. The troops marched steadily. An ominous silence reigned everywhere ; not even a Mexican scout was to be seen.

Several miles from Goliad Fannin halted an hour in the open prairie to allow his jaded and hungry ox-teams to graze. At the moment the march was taken up, a line of Mexican cavalry came out of the wood skirting the Colita (Co-lee′ta) Creek two miles away. Their arms glistened in the sunlight, for the fog had lifted. A compact mass of infantry followed. Urrea's entire army was upon them.

Fannin immediately formed his men in a hollow square with the wagons and teams in the center. His position had the double disadvantage of being unprotected and in a miry hollow some feet below the surface of the prairie around. But his men received the Mexican advance with a volley from the artillery and a galling fire from their rifles.[1]

The cannon, for want of water to sponge them, soon became useless. With small arms alone, charge after charge of the enemy was repulsed; the prairie was soon covered with dead and dying men and horses.

Early in the action Fannin received a severe wound in his thigh, but in spite of this he continued to direct his men with great courage and coolness.

Many a poor fellow loaded and fired his gun with his own life-blood wetting the sod about him. One lad, named Hal Ripley, fifteen years of age, after his thigh was broken by a ball, climbed, with Mrs. Cash's help, into her cart. There, with his back propped and a rest for his rifle, he fired away calmly until another bullet shattered his right arm. He had, in the meantime, killed four Mexicans. "Now, Mother Cash," he said cheerfully, "you may take me down."[2]

---

[1] This battle, called by the Mexicans the battle of the Encinal del Perdido, began at one o'clock P.M.

[2] Eleazer Wheelock Ripley, the father of Hal Ripley, was a brigadier-general in the United States army, and greatly distinguished himself in the war with Great Britain in 1812. He was afterward a member of the United States Congress from Louisiana.

GOLIAD.

At dark the Mexicans ceased firing and made their camp in the timber. Their bugles sounded shrilly the livelong night. That night was one of agony in the bloody little camp on the prairie. There were but seven Texans killed, but more than sixty were badly wounded. These groaned in the darkness, begging for water which could not be had, imploring aid which mortal hand was powerless to give. Those who were not wounded lay breathless and exhausted on the trampled ground, staring up at the sky and wondering what the morrow would bring forth.

The morrow brought no help to them. To the already large force of Urrea it brought reinforcements to the number of three or four hundred men with artillery, ammunition, and supplies.

Fannin watched the enemy ranging his men under the morning sky and dragging his cannon into place; then his haggard eyes sought his own brave little band. They were without food, drink, or ammunition; their teams were killed or disabled; their cannon were useless; the cries of their wounded rose mournfully on the heavy air. He called his officers together and submitted the question: " Shall we surrender or not?" The private soldiers were then asked to decide for themselves.

During this consultation Mrs. Cash went to the Mexican camp to beg for water for the wounded men. She was accompanied by her son, a boy of fourteen years, who, like Hal Ripley, had fought the day before with the best and the bravest. They passed over the prairie strewn with the dead and dying, and entered the presence of the Mexican general. " I have come, sir," she said, fearlessly, " to ask you before the fighting begins again, to give me water for our wounded." Urrea looked at her without replying, and then his eyes fell upon the shot-pouch and powder-horn of the boy. " Woman," he demanded sternly, " are you not ashamed to bring a child like that into such scenes?" The boy himself answered with his blue eyes kindling : " Young as I am, sir," he said, " I know my rights, as everybody in Texas does, and I mean to have them or die."

What the general might have said in answer to this insolent speech cannot be known, for at that moment a white flag was raised in the Texan camp.

The majority of Fannin's men were in favor of surrender, though many thought in their hearts it would be better to die with arms in their hands like the defenders of the Alamo. Fannin himself was opposed to surrender. "We beat them off yesterday," he declared, "and we can do it again to-day."

Favorable terms were secured from General Urrea by Fannin, and the prisoners of war were marched back to Goliad and placed in the mission church — Fannin's Fort Defiance. The wounded were brought in the next day and housed in the barracks; and several days later Ward and his men were thrust into the overcrowded church.

The prisoners were ill fed and badly treated. But when the first shock of their defeat had passed, they began to look forward eagerly to their release. They were told that they were to be placed at once on ships and sent to New Orleans, where they would be paroled and set at liberty.

On the Saturday evening after their capture, the sounds of gay laughter echoed from the time-stained walls of the chapel. The men sang " Home, Sweet Home," to the music of a flute played by one of their number. Fannin talked of his wife and children far into the night.

The next day was Palm Sunday.

In the old days of the mission, the Indian converts were accustomed on Palm Sunday to walk up the aisles of the church bearing green branches in their hands, in memory of Christ's entry into Jerusalem ; and hymns of joy and praise mingled with the incense which arose from the altar.

At just the sunrise hour, when in those old times the converts came carrying their dewy sweet-smelling boughs from the forest, the prisoners were awakened by their guards and marched out of the church. They were formed into four divisions and hurried away under various pretences. Some were even told that they were starting home.

Three-quarters of a mile from the fort they were halted, drawn up in sections, and ordered to kneel. Everything had been so orderly, so natural, so swift, that only at the last moment did the men realize what was about to happen. "My God, boys," cried a voice that echoed like a shot on the clear air, "they are going to kill us."

The guns of the guards were already turned upon the prisoners. A deliberate discharge followed this despairing cry; another, and another, and a heap of writhing, bleeding bodies was all that remained of Fannin's gallant band. A few escaped, struggling to their feet and fleeing to the swamp pursued by shots and curses. The surgeons and one or two others were saved by the kindness of Colonel Garay, a Mexican officer.[1] One of these, Dr. Shackelford, captain of the Red Rovers, heard the firing as he entered the tent of his preserver. He did not know that anything had gone wrong; but he trembled and turned pale, and well he might! For three of his young nephews and his own son were among the killed.

Señora Alvarez, a Mexican woman, concealed several prisoners until after the massacre, and afterward helped them to escape. It was her tears and entreaties which moved Colonel Garay to risk keeping the surgeons in his tent. While the butchery was going on, she stood in the plaza, with her black hair streaming over her shoulders; and with flashing eyes she denounced Santa Anna and called down the vengeance of heaven upon his head. When she learned that Dr. Shackel-

[1] Colonel Garay was a native of Greece.

ford's son had been shot, she burst into tears and cried out, "Oh, if I had only known, I would have saved him."

Her husband was one of Urrea's officers, and her kindness to the Texan prisoners throughout the war ought never to be forgotten. "Her name," writes one of the survivors of the massacre, "should be written in letters of gold."

The two brave boys, Harry Ripley and young Cash, were also among the slain.

The wounded men were then dragged out of their beds and shot. Fannin, who was the last to die, met his fate inside the fort, it is even said inside the consecrated church. His high courage sustained him to the end. After receiving the promise of the officer in charge that he should not be shot in the head, that his body should be decently buried, and that his watch should be sent to his wife, he fastened the bandage about his eyes with his own hands, and welcomed death like a soldier. Not one of the promises made to him was kept.

The dead Texans to the number of three hundred and fifty were stripped of their clothing and piled, naked, in heaps on the ground. A little brushwood was thrown over them and set on fire. It burned, crackling a few moments, and then the flames died out. The half-consumed flesh was torn from the bones by vultures.

This cold-blooded murder was done by order of Santa Anna. For it, as for the massacre at the Alamo, a deadly vengeance was at hand.

5. REMEMBER THE ALAMO! REMEMBER GOLIAD!

On the morning of the 21st of April, 1836, Houston, with his army of seven hundred Texans, and Santa Anna, with his army of more than twice that number of Mexicans, were encamped within a mile of each other near the banks of Buffalo Bayou.

The country was in a wild panic. Men, women, and children were fleeing before the very rumor of Santa Anna's approach, as in the pioneer days they had not fled before the tomahawks of the Comanches.

Houston's slow retreat [1] (begun on March 13), from Gonzales to the Colorado, from the Colorado to various points on the Brazos, with the enemy close upon his rear, had filled the stoutest hearts with doubt and alarm. After more than two months of suspense charged with the terrible episodes of San Patricio, Refugio, the Alamo, and Goliad, and the burning of San Felipe, Gonzales, and Harrisburg, the people began to ask of each other what would be the end.

Here at last, on an open field and in a fair fight, the question was about to be answered.

Santa Anna, after the fall of the Alamo, was filled with vain glory. He called himself the Napoleon of the West, and looked upon the Texan "rebels" as already conquered and suppliant at his feet. From his headquarters at San Antonio he directed his army to possess the country and to shoot every man taken with a gun in his hand. One division, under General Gaona, was ordered to Nacogdoches; General Urrea, after the battle of Colita, was ordered to sweep the coast from Victoria to Anahuac with his division; the central division, under Generals Sesma and Filisola, followed Houston almost step by step in his retreat. Santa Anna himself accompanied this division.

On the 15th of April, believing that Houston was at last in

[1] Houston left Gonzales, March 13. Reached Burnham's Crossing, on the west bank of the Colorado, March 17. Crossed to the east bank of the Colorado and marched down to Beason's Crossing, March 19. Reached San Felipe on the Brazos, March 28. Marched up the Brazos (west bank) to Mill's Creek and Groce's Landing. Remained at Groce's Landing until April 12. Crossed the Brazos (April 12) to Groce's Plantation. Marched on the 14th; reached Buffalo Bayou, opposite Harrisburg, on the 18th. Crossed the same day in pursuit of Santa Anna. Occupied the battlefield of San Jacinto, April 20.

his power, the Mexican commander-in-chief left his main army on the Brazos and marched, with about one thousand men, to Harrisburg, where he hoped to capture President Burnet and the members of his cabinet. He found Harrisburg deserted; whereupon he set fire to the town, and hurried to New Washington. From there, after burning the straggling village, he intended to move on to Lynch's Ferry (now Lynchburg) at the junction of Buffalo Bayou and the San Jacinto River. His plan was to pursue the government officials to Galveston, whither they had retreated, make them prisoners, and so end the war. While his troops were in line for the ferry (April 20) he was startled by the arrival of a scout who reported the approach of Houston with his entire command. Santa Anna, thus cut off from his army, was taken completely by surprise.

Deaf Smith.

This was the moment Houston had so long awaited.

"We need not talk," he said to Rusk, the Secretary of War, who was with the army. "You think we ought to fight, and I think so, too."

GOLIAD.

The rising sun of April 21 looked down bright and glowing upon the two hostile camps. The Texans were in a grove of moss-hung live oaks; in front of them a rolling prairie, gay with spring flowers, stretched away to the marshy bottom lands of the San Jacinto River; behind them Buffalo Bayou rolled its dark waters to Galveston Bay. The "Twin Sisters," two small cannon presented to the Republic by the citizens of Cincinnati, were planted on the rising ground before the camp.

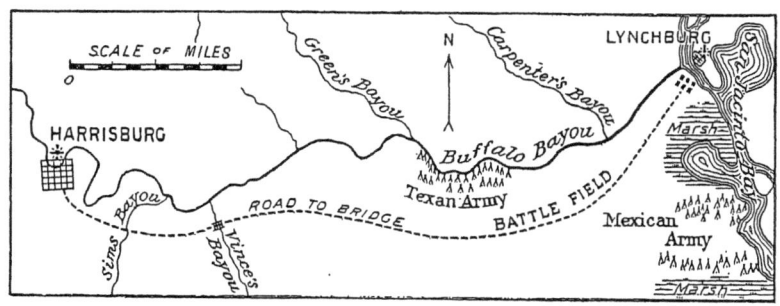

Battlefield of San Jacinto.

They were flanked on either side by the infantry. The cavalry, under the command of Mirabeau B. Lamar, was placed in the rear.

Santa Anna's camp also faced the prairie, but it had directly in the rear the oozy, grass-grown San Jacinto marsh.

The day before (20th) when the ground was first occupied by the two armies, there had been some skirmishing. But this morning passed in a quiet, which was broken only by the arrival of General Cos at the enemy's camp with a reinforcement of five hundred men.

Toward noon a profound silence fell upon the Mexican camp. The men, officers and soldiers, from Santa Anna to the humblest private, were taking their *siesta* (afternoon nap).

Meantime, General Houston, after a short consultation with his officers, sent for Deaf Smith.

Deaf Smith was a bold, cool-headed, shrewd guide and spy, who had come from New York to Texas in 1821. He was hard of hearing (hence his nickname), silent and secretive in his manner, with the instinct and the unerring sight of a savage. It was Deaf Smith who had guided Fannin and Bowie from La Espada to Mission Concepcion, and led Johnson and Milam through the dark streets at the storming of San Antonio. It was he who had been sent to meet Mrs. Dickinson on her dreary journey from the Alamo; and when General Houston retreated from Gonzales, Deaf Smith, with one or two companions, was left to spy upon the movements of the enemy.

Houston dispatched Smith with secret orders to cut down and burn Vince's bridge, about eight miles distant.

This bridge, which both armies had crossed on their march to their present position, spanned Vince's Bayou, a narrow but deep stream running into Buffalo Bayou. To destroy it was to destroy the only means of retreat for either army.

General Houston, after making these arrangements, paraded his army. The men were in high spirits. Their eyes were dancing, their fingers itched to pull the triggers of their guns. The day was waning; it was nearly three o'clock in the afternoon. At this moment Deaf Smith galloped in, his horse white with foam, with the news that Vince's bridge had been burned.

The order to advance was given. A single fife struck up the curiously inappropriate tune, "Will you come to the bower I have shaded for you." The cannon were rushed forward within two hundred yards of the Mexican camp, and fire belched from the mouth of the "twins." The left wing of infantry under Colonel Sidney Sherman began the attack. There was a cry which split the air: "Remember the Alamo! Remember Goliad!" and the whole force hurled itself forward like an avalanche.

The effect was appalling. The Mexicans half awake, dazed and bewildered by the sudden charge, hardly tried after their first feeble volley, to return the fire of their assailants. Within a few moments the Texans, still uttering their hoarse watchword of vengeance, had leaped the barricade, and were in the very heart of Santa Anna's camp.

Too excited or too thirsty for revenge to load, they beat down the foe with the butts of their rifles, clubbed them with pistols, slashed them with keen-edged bowie knives. The Mexicans fled like frightened sheep, some into the muddy morass where they were caught as in a trap, others toward the bayou and the ruined bridge, others again to the cover of the timber where they made haste to surrender. "Me no Alamo! Me no Alamo!" cried many of the panic-stricken soldiers, falling on their knees before their captors.

Sidney Sherman.

By twilight the fleeing Mexicans were nearly all captured or killed, and the victors had time to breathe and to count their own dead. They had seven dead and twenty-seven wounded. Among the latter was General Houston, who received a wound in the ankle, which caused him to limp during the remainder of his life.

The Mexicans lost six hundred and thirty-two killed and two hundred and eight wounded. Seven hundred and thirty-two prisoners were taken.

Among the prisoners were the oath-breaker, General Cos;[1] Almonte, Santa Anna's private secretary; and Colonel Portillia, the officer who had been in command at Goliad when

---

[1] Cos was Santa Anna's brother-in-law.

Fannin and his men were shot. General Santa Anna, riding a handsome black horse, had escaped. He was pursued as he fled from the field by Henry Karnes, who knew from the flying horseman's glittering uniform that he must be an officer of rank; he did not dream, however, that he was following Santa Anna. He felt sure of capturing the officer at Vince's Bayou, for he rode straight for the destroyed bridge. But after a single second of hesitation on the bank, the horse and rider seemed to rise in the air and then plunge downward. When Captain Karnes reached the stream, the gallant animal was floundering in the mud on the opposite side, unable to clamber up the steep bank. The rider had disappeared.

6. TWO GENERALS.

The next morning (22nd) General Houston was lying under an oak somewhat apart from the camp. The pain of his wound had kept him awake during the night, and he was sleeping lightly. Suddenly an excited murmur ran through the camp, a clamor of Mexican voices arose: "El Presidente! El Presidente!" and some soldiers approached, having in their midst a man dressed in soiled linen trousers, a blue jacket, a soldier's cap, and red worsted slippers. His linen, however, was of the finest, and he wore jeweled studs in his shirt front.

Houston, awakened by the noise, looked up. His visitor bowed. "I am," he said in Spanish, "General Antonio Lopez de Santa Anna, and a prisoner of war, at your service." He had just been captured, hiding, miserable and forlorn, in the long grass on the further side of the bayou. Houston waved his hand to a tool-chest near by, and Santa Anna sat down.

A greater physical contrast can hardly be imagined than that between these two men now gazing steadily and silently at each other.

The Dictator of Mexico was small and thin and not above five feet five inches in height. His swarthy face was ill-favored almost to repulsiveness; his small black eyes were cold and cruel. Houston was tall and finely proportioned, with fair complexion, open forehead, and fine blue eyes. Perhaps the one point of resemblance between the two generals lay in a certain foppishness in dress. But on this occasion this appeared in neither. Santa Anna had exchanged his gaudy uniform for the disguise he wore, and Houston was ill-kempt and shabby in his old campaign uniform.

Almonte, who had been sent for to act as interpreter, now came up and the interview began. Santa Anna was at first very humble; he even wept copiously. But after swallowing some opium he recovered his arrogance, and demanded to be treated as a prisoner of war. He wished to arrange for his immediate release.

When Houston dryly asked what consideration he could expect after the bloody scenes at the Alamo and Goliad, he pleaded the usage of war for the carnage at the Alamo. As for Goliad, he declared that Urrea had deceived him with regard to Fannin's surrender, and pretended to denounce his subordinate officer in bitter terms. " Urrea told me Fannin was vanquished," he said, "and I was ordered by my government to shoot every man found with a weapon in his hand."

" You are yourself the government," Houston replied curtly. " A Dictator has no superior."

" I have the order of Congress," Santa Anna insisted, "and that compels me to treat as pirates all who are found under arms. Urrea had no authority to make an agreement with Fannin. He has deceived me, and when I am free he shall suffer for it."

Houston listened to this bluster, but declined to make terms with his prisoner, that power belonging alone to the Texan Congress.

He treated the unfortunate general with generous courtesy, returning to him his tents and personal effects, and permitting him to be waited upon by his own servants.

An order signed by Santa Anna was carried by Deaf Smith and Henry Karnes to General Filisola, the second in command, who was encamped near San Felipe, to conduct the Mexican troops to the Rio Grande.

The Texan soldiers could not understand the mercy shown to the Mexican prisoners, particularly to Santa Anna, the cruel and heartless foe who had tortured and put to death so many of their brave countrymen. With dark and angry looks and open threats they swarmed about the place of the interview. Some of the officers were in favor of a drumhead court-martial and an immediate execution. But better counsels prevailed, and Santa Anna was allowed to retire to his camp-bed and rest in peace.

The night which followed the victory was one of wild and grotesque rejoicing in the Texan camp. Huge bonfires were lighted, and by the red glow of their flames, the soldiers danced and sang and told over and over again the story of the great day and its triumphs. The Mexican camp was overhauled; the victors decked themselves with the arms of their foes, buckling about their waists two, three, or four brace of pistols, with powder-horns, shot-pouches, sabers, and bowie knives. They rigged out the captured mules with the gold epaulets of the Mexican officers, and the green and red cap-cords of the grenadiers. Then, lighting hundreds of wax candles found among the spoils, they paraded gayly about, waking the echoes of the night with their shouts of laughter. All this was not in very good taste, and it naturally made the prisoners very angry. But they might well have reflected that at least it was a better way of rejoicing over a victory than shooting prisoners in cold blood and setting fire to their naked corpses.

The military stores taken in the battle, the cannon, small arms, ammunition, and mules, were kept by the government.

The camp baggage was sold at auction, and the proceeds, with the contents of the military money-chest, were divided among the soldiers. This money, which amounted to about seven dollars and a half to each man, was all that they received for their service during the whole war.

General Santa Anna's handsome silver-mounted saddle was purchased and presented to General Houston. The jeweled dagger handed to his captors by the Mexican General was also given to Houston.

7. HOW THE GOOD NEWS WAS BROUGHT.

On the approach of Santa Anna's army, President Burnet and his cabinet retired from Harrisburg to Galveston Island. They were closely pressed by the advance of the Mexican cavalry under Almonte. As the President stepped upon the flat-boat which was to take him to the schooner *Flash*, at the mouth of the San Jacinto, he was for several moments a target for Mexican guns. But he reached the *Flash* in safety, and the boat sailed across the bay to the almost deserted island. There, while the government officials waited in great anxiety and suspense for news from the army, they were joined by a large number of fugitives who had fled from their homes in the general panic. The steamboat *Yellowstone* — which had conveyed Houston's army across the Brazos at Groce's Ferry — came down loaded with refugees from the Brazos and Colorado. At Fort Bend it had passed the Mexican army under a hot fire. The smokestacks were riddled with bullet holes. The Mexican cavalrymen had tried at several points to lasso the boat from the bank as it steamed by, but fortunately their ropes were too short.

The *Yellowstone* brought news that Houston's army was on the road to Harrisburg. Burnet knew, therefore, that the long-delayed fight would take place soon or never. Very few people had any faith left in Houston's ability to defeat the Mexican army. Santa Anna was looked for in Galveston at any moment. Nearly all the women and children had already been placed on board the *Flash*, and the captain of the boat had orders to sail for New Orleans, where they would be safe.

General Houston's first duty, after settling affairs in his somewhat disordered camp, was to send an express to the President with news of the victory, and to request him to come and treat in person with Santa Anna.

At the battle of Concepcion Captain Robert Calder, then a private posted in the mission tower, had given notice of the enemy's approach. This young officer, who had also fought most gallantly in the battle of San Jacinto, volunteered to bear the General's dispatches to President Burnet. It is not to the young captain's discredit that the presence on the island of the beautiful girl whom he afterward married had something to do with his eagerness to perform this service.

Thomas J. Rusk.

He started on the morning of the 23d accompanied by B. C. Franklin and two soldiers detailed for the expedition. No boat was to be had except an open and weather-stained skiff with two pairs of oars. No provisions could be procured; the country around had been swept clean by the Mexicans. But the little party paddled away cheerily down the bayou. Late at night they found some food in a deserted cabin on the bank. The next day they entered the bay. The waves were rough; it was hard rowing and the boat leaked badly. Captain Calder had most of the work to do, the others having given out completely. Much of the way they coasted close to the shore, Calder wading and shoving or pulling the skiff along. They saw but one living human being on their trip. This was a wild African negro who had perhaps escaped from some slave-ship on the coast. On the fifth day they crossed from Virginia Point to the war-schooner *Invincible*, which was lying in the bay off Galveston. As they approached, Captain Brown hailed them through his speaking trumpet: "What news?"

The unexpected reply, "Houston has defeated Santa Anna and captured his whole army," caused an instant outburst of wild excitement. The wet, weary, and hungry messengers were dragged on board and questioned by everybody at once. Captain Brown cried to his gunners: "Turn loose old Tom." Old Tom, the cannon, was fired three times before Captain Brown remembered that it was the business of the Commodore to order a salute. "Hold on there, boys," he said, "or old Hawkins will have me in irons."

He sent Captain Calder and his men over to the flag-ship *Independence*, where Commodore Hawkins received them with enthusiasm and ordered a salute of thirteen guns.

The news spread among the ships and through the fleet of small boats that swarmed up to hear the story. It passed on to the land, where people were running about in a wild state of alarm at the sound of the commodore's guns. Alarm was changed to joy. The refugees hugged each other, weeping tears of gladness, and fairly beside themselves with delight. President Burnet received Captain Calder in his tent and heard the story of the battle with deep emotion.

The young captain, "having changed his clothes," as he relates, went in search of the bright-eyed girl whom he had not seen since the war began. As he passed, unknown, through the groups of men, he heard one man exclaim: "What! the whole Mexican army defeated and Santa Anna taken prisoner?

No, gentlemen; these fellows are scoundrels and deserters. It is too big a story, and they ought to be taken into custody at once."

President Burnet and his suite boarded the *Yellowstone* the same day (April 27) and steamed up to the new camp near Harrisburg, whither Houston had removed his army. There he met Santa Anna and arranged the basis of a treaty which the Mexican general signed on the part of his country.

By the terms of the treaty the Mexican army was to withdraw from Texas soil; hostilities were to cease; American prisoners were to be released; and all property seized during the invasion was to be returned to the owners. Santa Anna was to be liberated at the discretion of the Congress.

On the 3d day of May the Mexican prisoners were placed on board the *Yellowstone* and carried to Galveston island, where they were kept under close guard.

President Burnet accompanied Santa Anna to the coast, whence it was intended to embark the Mexican general at once for Vera Cruz.

Soon after the battle of San Jacinto, General Houston, leaving Rusk, who had recently been appointed brigadier-general, in command of the army, went to New Orleans to have his shattered ankle treated by his own physician.

Filisola had heard of the defeat and capture of his commander-in-chief and was already in full retreat when Santa Anna's order reached him. He arrived at Goliad about the 20th of May.

Here, on the 26th, Commissioners Benjamin Fort Smith and Henry Teal found him. They had been sent by President Burnet with a copy of the treaty between Santa Anna and the Texan congress for Filisola's signature. He signed it, and continued his march westward to the Rio Grande.

On June 4 General Rusk — who had followed with the Texan army to see that the Mexicans retreated in good faith — stopped at Goliad to fulfill a sacred duty. This was to collect and bury the remains of the victims of the Palm Sunday massacre.

The charred and sun-dried skeletons scattered about the ground were gathered together and reverently laid in a pit dug for the purpose. The army was paraded inside the fort, and

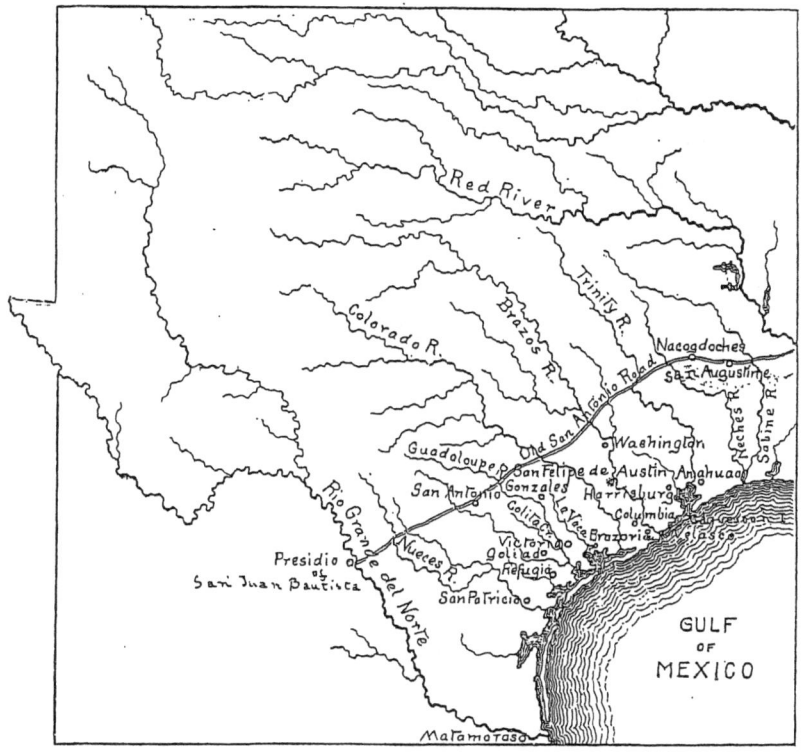

Map of Texas at the Close of the War of Independence.

from thence, slowly and with reversed arms, to the beat of muffled drums, the soldiers marched to the chosen spot. With the procession walked several of Fannin's men who had escaped death on that fatal Sunday.

General Rusk began an address, the troops standing around him. "But in truth he did not finish what he intended to say, for he was overpowered by his feelings, and the tears rolled down his cheeks, and he had to stop speaking. There were but few dry eyes on that occasion." [1]

So powerful was the impression produced on the men who assisted in this mournful ceremony that General Andrade (An-dra'dā), who was bringing up the rear of the Mexican army, was advised by Rusk that it would not be safe for him to attempt to pass through Goliad, as he could not answer for what his own men might do. Andrade was therefore obliged to cut a crossing seven or eight miles long through the chapparal thickets, in order to reach the main road. The Mexican army marched slowly westward with trailing banners. San Antonio and other places held by Mexican garrisons were given up. At length the Rio Grande was reached and crossed.

The independence of Texas was achieved.

[1] Moses Bryan, in *Texas Scrap Book.*

VI.

HOUSTON.

(1836-1842.)

1. ON BUFFALO BAYOU.

The treaty between Santa Anna and the Texan Congress was concluded at Velasco (May 14), and to the written paper was affixed the seal of the Republic.

The choice of this seal was the result of an accident. When the declaration of independence was adopted at San Felipe, Governor Smith, having no other seal, used one of the brass buttons from his coat. Its device chanced to be a five-pointed star encircled by a wreath of oak leaves. The Lone Star with its wreath thus became the official signet of the Texas Republic.

Santa Anna was conducted on board the war-schooner *Invincible*, which had orders to convey him and his staff to Vera Cruz on the coast of Mexico. But public feeling was so strong against setting free the arch enemy of Texas that President Burnet was obliged to have him brought on shore again. He was sent from Velasco to Columbia, and thence to Orizaba, the country place of Dr. Orlando Phelps, on the Brazos River. A plot for his release was soon afterward discovered. This caused him to be put in irons, and to receive a small taste of

Flag of Texas Republic.

the ill-treatment he had so often accorded to others. It was not until after the return of Houston from New Orleans in the fall that the captive general was finally released.

Meantime there was great dissatisfaction in the army. The soldiers, having no fighting to do, began to remember that they were hungry and in rags. They clamored for money which the poverty-stricken government could not give them; and they still demanded loudly the death of Santa Anna.

In June Major Isaac Burton, with a company of mounted rangers on the lookout for Mexican vessels at Copano, succeeded in decoying into port and capturing three supply ships which belonged to the enemy. These were the *Watchman*, the *Comanche*, and the *Fanny Butler*. The supplies, valued at twenty-five thousand dollars, were sent at once to the army. This timely relief and the re-imprisonment of Santa Anna restored the soldiers to good humor.

In September a general election was held. General Houston was made President, and Mirabeau B. Lamar Vice-President. The new term was to begin in December; but President Burnet, glad to lay down the burden which he had borne wisely and virtuously, resigned his office, and on the 22d of October Houston was inaugurated.

The ceremony took place at Columbia. Among those present were many who had been prominent in the revolution: Stephen F. Austin, ex-Governor Smith, Branch T. Archer, the Whartons, Mosely Baker, Sidney Sherman, John T. Austin, William Austin, and many others.

Santa Anna, in his guarded apartment not far away, might almost have heard the echoes of his old enemy's voice when, at the conclusion of his address, Houston unbuckled his sword and handed it to the Speaker of the House, with the assurance that if his country should ever call for his services again he would resume his sword and respond to that call with his blood or his life.

Stephen F. Austin was made Secretary of State in Houston's cabinet. He had but lately returned from the United States, where he had rendered important service to Texas during her struggle for independence. He now saw his highest hopes realized. His beloved colonists had become a free people. His chosen land would now blossom like a rose in the fair sunshine of peace.

He began his new duties with ardor. But constant anxiety and the hardships of prison life had left him weak and delicate. The unfinished room where he worked was without fire; he was seized suddenly with pneumonia, and after a short illness he died (December 27, 1836).

The Father of Texas was but forty-three years old. His life had been noble, useful, and unselfish, and his death was a public loss. His body was conveyed in the steamer *Yellowstone* to Peach Point on the Brazos, near Columbia. There, in the

Mirabeau B. Lamar.

presence of the President and his cabinet, the officers of the army and navy, and a large concourse of citizens, he was buried with military honors.

The first regular Congress had a hard task before it. The people of Texas were in favor of annexation to the United States. But a strong faction in that nation, though willing to acknowledge Texas as an independent country, was strongly opposed to receiving another slave state. The young Republic was therefore obliged to stand alone.

There was a large public debt, but no money in the treasury.

Mexico still laid claim to her rebellious province, and it was necessary to maintain an army to repel invasion, and a navy to defend the coast. The Indians were troublesome. The civil law, in the confusion and disorder of the war, had become almost a dead letter.

This was a tangled skein, but Congress set to work with hearty good will to unravel the threads. The legislature pro-

First Capitol of Texas. At Columbia (1836).

vided for the public debt and other state expenses by issuing land scrip (government paper entitling the holder to so many leagues of land).

County and magistrate courts were organized; a Supreme Court was formed, and the Spanish code of laws was displaced by the code used by the United States. The soldiers instead of their pay received permission to go home on long visits to their families. Some vessels were bought for the navy, and commissioners were sent to the different Indian tribes to make treaties of friendship.

Congress adjourned in December. The following May it met in the new town on Buffalo Bayou named in honor of the President.

Monsieur Le Clère (Le Clare), a Frenchman who visited Texas about this time, writes thus of Houston : " I cannot say that Houston is a great city, although it is a capital. The principal street, Main Street, which is laid out in a straight line, and handsome enough for the country, runs down to the river. The footwalks are barely marked out. We found the landing still blocked by enormous trunks of trees. Great southern pines are left standing in the street. The ascent which leads from the bayou to the city is very rough, and one stumbles over the logs that encumber it. By the side of houses of tolerably fine appearance (though built entirely of wood), one meets here and there with those poor houses called log cabins. Finally, as a last touch to this picture, there stand in Main Street and near the capitol two great tents which would do honor to a chief of the Tartars or Bedouins.

"The environs of Houston are not inhabited. A great number of the people I saw in the city were going further west, but their passage gave it a very lively appearance. They were on horseback, and almost all armed with the terrible weapon called the bowie knife. Most of them carried before them on the saddle that rifle, excessively long, which they handle with a wonderful skill, and which Jackson's men used so well at the battle of New Orleans."

The capitol building was unfinished, and Congress was obliged to shorten its sittings when it rained or a "norther" blew fiercely through the shutterless windows. The President's house was a double log cabin with a puncheon floor. But the naturalist Audubon describes President Houston (May, 1837) as receiving his guests in this rude cabin, "dressed in a fancy velvet coat and trousers trimmed with gold lace; and around his neck was tied a cravat somewhat in the style of 1776."

The same writer speaks of the members of the cabinet as men bearing the stamp of "intellectual ability, simple, though bold in their general appearance."

All sorts of people from at home and abroad thronged the little capital. Curious travelers like Audubon and Le Clère, the Frenchman, brushed against hunters clad in buck-skin, traders with pack-mules, and eager-eyed young adventurers from "the States."

A Comanche Chief.

A great many Indians came into the town to see their Great Father, Houston. One such deputation was from the hunting-grounds of the Comanches. They came to make their treaty of peace in person. They rode mustang ponies, and brought their squaws and papooses with them. After setting up their buffalo-hide lodges on the prairie near the town, the warriors marched in single file to President Houston's own residence. They were all tall and finely formed, with very red skin, and jet-black hair which they wore hanging in long locks down their backs. These locks were ornamented with bands of silver. Many of the warriors wore, just below the elbow, clumsy rings of copper or gold, from which dangled the scalp-locks of their dead enemies. Monsieur Le Clère, who saw this procession, says that one young Indian had two of these rings hung with ten or fifteen heads of hair of different colors. The women wore tight leggings of tanned buck-skin, with tunics of wolf or jaguar skins, trimmed with beads and quills. Many strands of colored beads were strung around their necks, and their hands were loaded with gold and silver rings. Some of their costumes were graceful and pretty. The wearers were nearly all old and ugly; but one young girl, the daughter of the chief, is described as very beautiful, with liquid black eyes, softly rounded cheeks, and red laughing lips. She wore on her head a crown made of eagle feathers, and her girdle was a band of heavy silver discs.

The President welcomed his red brothers gravely and kindly. The calumet, or pipe of peace, was smoked and the treaty was made. The Indians received presents of beads, blankets, and red cloth. The old chief when he rode away carried the Texas flag tied to a stalk of sugar cane. "Me big chief! Houston big chief!" he cried, striking his breast with his hand.

2. THE INVINCIBLE.

The provisional government of 1835 provided for a navy to serve the new Republic of Texas. It was not a very formidable navy. It consisted at first of two vessels — the schooners the *Invincible* and the *Liberty*. Afterward were added the *Independence*, which became the flag-ship of Commodore Hawkins, commandant of the fleet, the *Brutus*, and several small sloops, including the *Champion* and the *Julius Cæsar*.

These ships cruised about the Gulf of Mexico, watching the coast and doing what they could with their small guns to annoy the Mexican war-vessels. Early in April, 1836, the *Invincible*, commanded by Captain Jerry Brown, met the Mexican brig, the *Montezuma*, near Tampico and fired upon her. A spirited engagement followed which lasted several hours, and in which the *Montezuma* was badly disabled. She drew off, and in attempting to enter the harbor ran aground.

The *Invincible* sailed away unhurt, and the next day met and captured the American brig, the *Pocket*, which was on her way to a Mexican port with a cargo of supplies for Santa Anna's army. Captain Brown brought the *Pocket* into Galveston, whence the supplies were forwarded to the army.

The *Invincible*, lying at that time in the bay, received from Captain Calder the first news of the victory at San Jacinto, and Captain Brown at once "turned loose Old Tom" to express his own joy therefor.

The *Yellowstone* came down from the Texan camp and landed the Mexican prisoners on the island; she then proceeded to Velasco, having on board the President and his cabinet officers, and General Santa Anna and his staff.

The *Invincible* was ordered to follow, and after signing the treaty, Santa Anna was conducted on board, and Captain Brown received orders to sail to Vera Cruz with the defeated general. The Texan commissioners empowered to treat with the Mexican government were also on board. As already related, Santa Anna was taken ashore again and placed in prison. The *Invincible* with the *Brutus* was soon afterward sent to New York for repairs. The *Liberty* conveyed General Houston to New Orleans, and was there sold to pay her war-expenses.

The new Congress was without means to meet the cost of repairing and refitting the *Invincible* and her sister ship. They were on the point of being sold when Henry Swartwout, the collector of the port of New York, with great generosity provided the money from his private purse. They were completely equipped and sent to sea the same year.

In 1837 the entire fleet set out for a cruise in the Gulf of Mexico. The *Champion* and the *Julius Cæsar* were taken by the enemy on the 12th of April. Both carried valuable cargoes, and their loss was a keen blow to the young government.

On the 17th of April the *Independence* encountered near Velasco two Mexican brigs of war, — the *Libertador*, armed with sixteen 18-pound guns and manned with one hundred and forty men, and the *Vincedor*, with six 12-pounders and

Old Capitol at Houston (1837). From an old Print.

one hundred men. The *Independence* had but thirty-one men. The action, in which the Texans behaved with great gallantry, was a short and severe one. It ended in the capture of the *Independence*. The crew were sent as prisoners to Matamoras.

A little later the *Invincible* and the *Brutus* captured the Mexican schooners, the *Obispo* and the *Telegraph*. Both boats were sent in as prizes.

In August the *Brutus* and the *Invincible* reached Galveston with another prize. The *Brutus* with the prize entered the harbor safely, but the *Invincible* did not succeed in passing the bar. She was attacked the next morning (26th) by two Mexican ships. The *Brutus* started out to assist her, but ran aground and lay helpless on the sand. The *Invincible* held her own against the enemy all day; at nightfall she struck on the breakers. Her crew were saved, but the gallant old ship went to pieces.

The next year (1838) a new navy was voted by Congress. Several vessels were bought, but there was now no duty for them to perform. They were placed in the service of Yucatan, which was in revolt against Mexico. Some years later, when Texas was annexed to the United States, they passed into the navy of that country.

The *Brutus*, the last ship of the old Texan navy, was lost in a storm at Galveston Bay as late as 1867.

3. THE CAPITAL.

One of the laws of the constitution provided that no one should be allowed to hold the office of President for two successive terms. Houston's term of office expired in 1838, and Mirabeau B. Lamar was elected President and David G. Burnet Vice-President.

The Secretary of War under Lamar was Albert Sidney Johnston. This brilliant young soldier came to Texas just after the battle of San Jacinto. He was a graduate of West Point, and had served in the Blackhawk war.

Johnston at once organized a force to act against the Indians. Lamar did not have Houston's kindly feeling for the Red Men. He looked upon them as dangerous enemies, and he wished to rid the country of them entirely. The Indians, on their side, had been breaking the treaties made with Houston.

Mexico was too full of troubles at home to invade Texas again. But Mexican agents were sent among the Cherokees and Comanches to stir them up against the white settlers, and incite them to reclaim their lands. Many homes on the frontier were burned, and their peaceable inmates killed or taken prisoners. The Texas rangers, under General Rusk and Colonel Burleson, finally defeated and subdued the most troublesome of the warlike tribes, and the frontier became quiet once more.

But in 1840 trouble broke out again with the Comanches.

First Executive Mansion. At Houston (1837).

Twelve chiefs of this tribe came to San Antonio to sign a new treaty. As usual, they were accompanied by their women and children. They had promised to bring with them thirteen white prisoners, but they appeared with but one, a little girl named Matilda Lockhart, who had been carried away in a raid on her father's house two years before. The chiefs declared they had no more prisoners. But the child said there were others at the camp, who were to be brought in one by one for large ransom. A company of soldiers was ordered into the council-room, and the Indians were told that they were prisoners until the other white captives were given up. One of the chiefs immediately attempted to escape, stabbing the sentinel at the door. A furious combat followed, in which the twelve chiefs were all killed. In the plaza outside there was also a desperate fight. The Indian women took part in this, and three of them were killed. Captain Matthew Caldwell, who was unarmed, defended himself with stones until his assailant was killed. Judge Thompson, who had been playing with the Indian children, setting up pieces of money for them to shoot at, was slain by an arrow from one of their bows. Colonel Wells came riding into the plaza in the midst of the skirmish. A powerful Indian leaped on his horse behind him and tried to shake him off. Unable to do this he seized the bridle and tried to guide the horse out of the plaza. Colonel Wells's arms were pinioned so that he could not draw his pistol, and it was only after careering thus several times around the plaza that the Indian was shot by a soldier and the Colonel released. The band was finally overpowered. Thirty-two warriors, three squaws, and two children were killed; the others were all made prisoners. This encounter is known as the "Council-house Fight."

Congress held its meetings in Houston until 1839. But the site for a new capital had been chosen. It was on the banks of the Colorado River, on the then extreme frontier. Two or three pioneer cabins already stood there, and the little settlement bore the proud name of Waterloo. But bands of savage Indians still roamed the hills and prairies adjacent. It was necessary to place guards about the grounds to protect the masons and carpenters while they were at work on the capitol building. Among the buildings erected was a block-house, as a refuge for the women and children in case of an Indian raid. The new capital was named Austin, in grateful memory of the Father of Texas.

Congress met at Austin for the first time in October, 1839.

Among the important acts of this session was the appropriation of fifty leagues of land for a state university, and three leagues to each county for schools.

This Congress also adopted a national flag, the same now used as the Texas state flag.

The first Lone Star flag was made at Harrisburg, and presented to a military company in 1835. The star was five-pointed, white, set on a ground of red. The flag raised by Fannin on the walls of Goliad when he heard of the declaration of independence was an azure star in a white field. Travis and his men, ignorant of the declaration, died fighting under the banner of the Republic of Mexico.[1]

England, France, Holland, and Belgium in turn recognized the independence of the Republic. Texas, in spite of many drawbacks, was growing in strength.

The last year of Lamar's term of office, however, was clouded by an unfortunate affair known as the "Sante Fé Expedition."

A scheme was set on foot for the occupation of New Mexico, whose people were said to be anxious to join the Texas Republic. Its real object was to divert into Texas the rich trade of Sante Fé with Old Mexico. An expedition was organized and started from Brushy Creek, near Austin, June, 1841. It was composed of about two hundred and seventy soldiers, together with a number of traders and adventurers. The soldiers were under the command of General Hugh McLeod.

Congress opposed this expedition, but President Lamar favored it, and sent with it three commissioners as agents of the government to treat with the people of New Mexico. General McLeod's brass six-pound cannon was stamped with he name of the President, Mirabeau B. Lamar.

The journey was a long and painful one. The men suffered from thirst in crossing those barren western plains, where

[1] Thrall.

water is scarce. They had nothing to eat. "Every tortoise and snake, every living and creeping thing was seized upon and swallowed by the famishing men."[1] They were without guides, and the Indians hung about their camps killing their pickets and stealing their horses.

When they reached New Mexico they were worn out and half starved. Instead of being welcomed as liberators they were looked upon as spies and enemies.

Under promise of good treatment they finally surrendered to the force sent against them. They were at once thrown into prison. Later they were sent, chained like criminals, to the city of Mexico. Several of them died on the march, unable to endure the brutality of their guards.

The survivors were held as prisoners in Mexican dungeons until the next year, when by the intervention of the American minister they were released and sent home.

4. THE WAR OF THE ARCHIVES.

Houston was elected President of the Republic for the second time in September, 1841. Edward Burleson was elected Vice-President.

The new President recommended economy to the government. There was not a dollar in the treasury. He caused his own salary to be reduced, and several useless offices were abolished by his advice. He favored a more friendly attitude toward the Indians, and the establishment of trading-posts for them on the frontier. He advised that no active steps be taken against Mexico, though Texas, he said, should be prepared to defend herself against that country if necessary.

For Santa Anna, after many turns of fortune, was once more in power in Mexico, and had declared war against Texas.

In the spring of 1842 several incursions were made into

[1] G. W. Kendall.

Texas by Mexican soldiers. One band, under Rafael Vasquez, raided San Antonio; another swept the country about Refugio and Goliad. There was great excitement everywhere.

Excitement of another kind filled the new capital one day soon after these raids. The citizens, men, women, and children, swarmed into the streets, looking at each other with indignant eyes. The blockhouse stood wide open, showing plainly that the Indians had nothing to do with the trouble.

"What's the matter?" demanded a tall hunter, who had just come in, rifle on shoulder, from the frontier. He glanced, as he spoke, from a small cannon in the street to a company of mounted rangers, who seemed to be guarding some wagons in front of the Land Office.

Texas State Seal.

"Matter enough," replied a dozen voices at once. "Old Sam Houston has changed the capital back to Houston and sent for the archives. We are determined that the records of the Republic shall remain in the true capital of the Republic."

This was true. President Houston, believing Austin in its exposed position was in danger of Mexican raids, had fixed Houston as the place of meeting for the next Congress. Perhaps he was not sorry for the chance, for he had a great affection for the town named for himself. He had also ordered the archives removed to that place. The people of Austin had refused to allow their removal. The angry President had then sent an armed force to take them.

When the loaded wagons turned away from the Land Office they were greeted by a volley of grape and canister from the little cannon — touched off by a woman, Mrs. Eberle. No one was hurt, and in the confusion the wagons rattled away, protected by their escort.

The citizens armed themselves and pursued the train. They came up with it during the night about eighteen miles from Austin. After a conference between the leaders on both sides, the rangers agreed to carry the records back to the capital. The whole party appeared there the next day and were received with shouts of triumph by the people. The disputed parchments were placed in the house of the plucky woman who had fired the cannon, and there they remained until 1845, when the government finally returned to Austin. This new Waterloo has come down to us under the title of the "War of the Archives."

Congress met at Houston in June, 1842. In September a Mexican army, commanded by General Adrian Woll and numbering twelve hundred men, invaded Texas. They marched upon San Antonio, captured it, and made prisoners of nearly all the citizens and the members of the District Court then in session.

Upon news of this outrage the people everywhere took up arms. Two hundred and twenty soldiers, including Captain Jack Hays' company of scouts, left Gonzales immediately to attack Woll. They were commanded by Colonel Matthew Caldwell. The Mexican general came out to meet them, and an engagement took place on the Salado River a few miles from San Antonio. General Woll had six hundred infantry and two hundred cavalry. As they advanced the Texans received them with a rattling hail of bullets.

Three times the Mexican infantry charged with great spirit and coolness; each time they were driven back. They finally retreated, carrying with them their dead and wounded, and leaving the Texans in possession of the field.

This victory was offset by the defeat of a company of fifty-three Texans on their way to join Caldwell. They were commanded by Captain Nicholas Dawson.

General Woll met these men in his retreat from the river Salado, and attacked them in a small mesquit thicket where they were halted. After an unequal contest of half an hour, Dawson hoisted a white flag. The firing ceased, but as soon as the surrender took place, the prisoners were set upon by the Mexican soldiers and many of them killed. Dawson was killed after he gave up his arms. Out of his fifty-three men, thirty-three were killed and eighteen were made prisoners. Two only escaped; one of these, a lad named Gonzales Woods, seized the lance thrust at him by a Mexican cavalryman, jerked his assailant to the ground, then leaped upon his enemy's horse and galloped away.

The morning after these skirmishes General Woll abandoned San Antonio and returned to the west side of the Rio Grande River. His prisoners, among whom were Judge Hutchison and ex-Lieutenant-Governor Robinson, were sent to the Castle of Perote (Pā-ro'tā), a prison near the city of Mexico.

5. THE BLACK BEANS.

Before the echoes of the bugles which sounded General Woll's retreat had finally died on the air, volunteers came flocking to San Antonio eager to pursue him, and determined to cross the Rio Grande at all hazards and release the Texans languishing in Mexican prisons.

On the 18th of November seven hundred men, armed and equipped for a campaign, were assembled in the shadow of the twin towers of the old Mission Concepcion. General Alexander Somervell, appointed by President Houston to the command, put himself at the head of this small army; the order to march ran down the line, and with a shout the men set their faces toward the west.

After several days' march they camped at Laredo on the banks of the Rio Grande River. They expected to cross at once into Mexico and take the enemy by surprise. But at the moment when everything seemed to them favorable for this movement, General Somervell issued an order for his soldiers to return to Gonzales, where they would be disbanded.

The men were dumfounded. Three hundred flatly refused to obey the order. The others, after much wrangling, followed General Somervell to San Antonio.

Captain William S. Fisher was elected colonel in command of those who remained, and the expedition proceeded down the Rio Grande to a point opposite the Mexican town of Mier.

Mier was occupied by General Pedro Ampudia (Am-poo'dee-a) with two thousand troops. On Christmas morning, before daylight, Colonel Fisher led his men over the river. The Mexicans came out to meet them, but were forced to retreat before the hot fire of the Texans. By daylight the Texans had captured the enemy's cannon and cut their way into the town. Here the fight went on, hand to hand, from street to street, from house to house.

But the superior numbers of the enemy enabled them to keep up the struggle, which lasted seventeen hours.

At the end of that time a flag of truce was sent by General Ampudia to Colonel Fisher. Fisher had been severely wounded early in the action; he was weakened by loss of blood and unnerved by pain; and he advised surrender, although up to this time his men had been victorious. He knew General Ampudia, he said, and he answered for his good faith.

After much discussion the majority of the men agreed to the surrender. The terms were most honorable.

No sooner were the articles signed and the Texan arms stacked, than the unfortunate prisoners began to suffer from the cruelty of their treacherous foes. They were put in irons and marched to Matamoras, thence to the interior. At the Hacienda of Salado, beyond Saltillo, they rose upon their guards, overpowered the soldiers, seized their weapons and horses, and escaped. But they found themselves in a strange country. They soon lost their way in the wild mountain passes, and after enduring great torture from hunger and thirst, they were finally recaptured and taken back to Salado.

On their arrival there they were met by an order from Santa Anna. Every tenth man of them was to be shot! One of their own number who understood Spanish was compelled to read this order to his companions. The rattle of handcuffs, indicating the surprise of the startled prisoners, was promptly silenced by the guards; and, amid a deadly stillness which succeeded the reading, an officer entered the shed where they were confined. He carried an earthen jar. The jar contained one hundred and seventy-five beans (the number of the prisoners). Seventeen of the beans were black, the others were white. The jar was placed on a bench and a handkerchief thrown over it. The roll was then called. Each prisoner stepped forward as his name was called, placed his hand in the jar, and drew out a bean.

The black beans in this fatal lottery meant death.

Some of the Mexican officers grew faint as they looked, and turned away their heads. But others bent forward eagerly, as if watching the throw of dice in an everyday game of chance.

It was Sunday afternoon, at the hour when the church bells were everywhere calling the people to vesper prayer, when this fearful drama began. Not one of the actors in it faltered or changed color at finding in his hand the black token of death. When the ordeal was ended, the shackles of the seventeen doomed men were knocked off. They were then hurried to a yard adjoining the shed and shot without further ceremony. Their comrades, crouched against the wall within, heard but too plainly the whispered prayers, the echoing shots, and the dying groans.

The survivors were carried to the Castle of Perote near the city of Mexico, where they found the prisoners taken by General Woll at San Antonio. They were immediately put to convict labor. "They were hitched to a wagon, twenty-five to a team, and compelled to haul rocks from the mountains to the Castle of Perote. The prisoners at no time, however, lost their buoyant spirits, nor did they ever lose an opportunity for fun. McFall, a powerful man, was put in the lead, and was always ready to get scared and run away with the wagon. This was often done, and the corners of the adobe houses always suffered in such cases. The Mexican officers would laugh, and the owners of the houses would swear in bad Spanish. The overseers were kept busy. They had the power of using the lash, but they did not do this very often, as the Texans made it their business, at the peril of their lives, to return such civilities with ample vengeance."[1]

Anson Jones.

Several of the prisoners made their escape. Among these was Colonel Thomas Jefferson Green, who had been Fisher's second in command. He was bitterly opposed to the surrender at Mier, and broke his sword across his knee rather than hand it to General Ampudia. Mr. John Twohig, of San Antonio, who had been carried into captivity by Woll, and several of his fellow-prisoners made a tunnel under the prison wall, through which they succeeded in getting out of the Castle and thence safe home again.

Mr. Wright of De Witt County was not so lucky. He was a very large man; after making his preparations for flight, he crawled into the tunnel, where he got along famously until he was about half way through. There he stuck fast, equally una-

[1] Quoted by Yoakum from a narrative by one of the prisoners.

ble to go forward or to come back. Finally, with a despairing effort he slid back an inch or two, then a little further, until at last bruised, breathless, and torn, he got back into his dungeon, glad to settle down to prison life once more.

Among the captives was Samuel H. Walker, afterwards famous as a captain of cavalry in the Mexican war with the United States.

In September, 1844, these prisoners were finally released by Santa Anna, at the dying request, it is said, of his young and beautiful wife.

About the time the Mier expedition started from San Antonio, the capital was again removed from President Houston's beloved town on Buffalo Bayou; this time to Washington on the Brazos.

VII.

AUSTIN.

(1842-1861.)

1. "THE REPUBLIC IS NO MORE."

From 1842 to 1844 the Texan Congress held its meetings at Washington on the Brazos — the spot where, a few short years before, the declaration of independence had been adopted.

The nation born amid the gloom and uncertainty of that stormy time now stood forth proud in the consciousness of growing strength, free and full of hope for the coming years.

An armistice was signed with Mexico (1843) which left the Republic at peace. The Indians under the wise rule of the "Big White Chief," Houston, made but few outbreaks. Year by year more fields were fenced in, more orchards and gardens were planted, more dooryards were set with vine and rose-tree.

Immigrants poured in. Many came from "the States"; but others crossed the wide seas to find homes in that fertile Texas whose story of struggle and triumph was in everybody's mouth. Henry Castro, a French gentleman, who was consul-general for Texas at Paris, obtained in 1842 large grants of land from the Republic, and brought over five hundred families from France. These settled on the Medina River west of San Antonio. Another important colony came from Germany under the leadership of the Prince de Solms, and founded the thrifty town of New Braunfels on the Guadalupe.

The roads were white with westward-traveling wagons which stopped to pass the time of day, as it were, with all the little towns along the way. In those hospitable days small barrels of tar stood as a matter of course on the sidewalks. Long-handled dippers floated in the tar, so that the passing wagoner might help himself and ease his creaking wheels.

As for the wayside houses, their doors were always open to the wayworn mover and his family. The women and girls

Old Capitol at Austin (1839).

peering out from under the wagon cover, the boys trudging sturdily along by the driver's side, the dog trotting in the shadow of the feed trough, — all these were to the free-handed pioneers as welcome as kinsmen.

The newcomers were often struck with amazement at the curious contrasts they saw on the frontier. "You are welcomed," writes one traveler, "by a figure in a blue flannel shirt and pendant beard, quoting the Latin poets. . . . You will see fine pictures on log walls ; you will drink coffee from tin cups on Dresden china saucers. Seated on a barrel, you will hear a Beethoven symphony played on a rosewood piano. The bookcase may be half full of books and half full of potatoes."

But while the western border thus filling up with settlers was quiet and unmolested, there was serious trouble over on the eastern line. A band composed mostly of rough desperadoes from the old Neutral Ground roamed along the Sabine River, shooting and killing innocent citizens under the pretext of punishing theft, negro-stealing, and other offenses. They called themselves the Regulators. An opposition band, made up of men as reckless as themselves, undertook in turn to punish them, and to administer justice generally. These were known as the Moderators. Between the Moderators and Regulators, Shelby, Harrison, and the neighboring counties were kept in a state of terror. Honest men were afraid to venture out of their own homes ; for no one could guess when or upon whom the so-called justice of these bands would fall. Bloody "courts" were held in the swamps, one day by the Regulators, the next, and perhaps on the same spot, by the Moderators, both equally cruel and lawless. Wild stories were told of certain leaders in either gang whose victims were always shot in the left eye ; of others again whose weapon was not the rifle, but poison.

At one time more than a thousand men were engaged in this feud. In the summer of 1844 the Regulators and Moderators assembled under arms in fortified camps. An active campaign was carried on for some weeks, during which more than fifty persons were killed or wounded. Finally President Houston ordered out five hundred militia under General James Smith, and the two factions were disbanded. But it was a long time before the feud died out entirely.

In the fall of 1844 Anson Jones was elected President of the Republic. His Secretary of State was Doctor Ashbel Smith.

Dr. Smith, who was a learned and able man, came to Texas from Connecticut just after the Revolution, and was made surgeon-general of the army. During Houston's administration, he represented the Republic at the courts of England and France. At this time all over Europe there was keen interest in Texan affairs.

Notwithstanding the glory of the young Republic, its people still wished to be annexed to the United States. They felt themselves too weak to contend against Mexico in case of another war, and too poor to keep up the army and navy, and provide for the expense of a separate government. But the United States again refused to receive them. Upon this, France and England offered through Minister Smith to compel Mexico to acknowledge the independence of Texas, provided Texas would agree not to unite with any other country.

This offer caused a sudden change of feeling in the United States. Her jealousy of foreign interference was aroused; and in the spring of 1845 the United States Congress passed resolutions admitting Texas into the Union.

President Jones then submitted the question to the people. A convention met at Austin in July, 1845, to frame a constitution for the State of Texas. In October the final vote was taken. It was almost unanimous for annexation.

In February, 1846, President Jones gave up his authority to J. Pinckney Henderson who had been elected governor of the new state. This impressive ceremony took place at Austin, where the capital had been finally established. President Jones in his farewell address said:

"The Lone Star of Texas, which ten years since arose amid clouds, over fields of carnage, and obscurely seen for a while, . . . has passed on and become fixed in that glorious constellation which all freemen and lovers of freedom must reverence and adore, — the American Union. Blending its rays with its sister States, long may it continue to shine. . . . May the Union be perpetual; and may it be the means of conferring benefits and blessings upon all the people of the States, is my prayer. The first act in the great drama is performed. The Republic of Texas is no more."[1]

Many eyes must have grown dim as the closing sentence of this address was pronounced. Memories must have crowded thick and fast upon those veterans who listened, hearing at the same time in a dream the call of bugles and the roll of drums, the ring of sabers, and the echo of those daring voices which called into being the Republic of Texas!

Sam Houston and Thomas J. Rusk were elected United States senators. Rusk, who was a native of South Carolina, was one of the signers of the Texan declaration of independence. He was Secretary of War under President Burnet, and fought gallantly in the ranks at the battle of San Jacinto. After General Houston's resignation he was made commander-in-chief of the army. Rusk had taken an active part in the war against the Cherokee Indians. Later he had been chief justice of the Republic. He had devoted himself for many years with great unselfishness to the interests of the Republic. He continued to serve the State with the same fidelity.

He died by his own hand in 1857. Grief at the death of his wife was the cause of this fatal act.

2. ACROSS THE BORDER.

Mexico was indignant at seeing Texas, which she still claimed as one of her provinces, about to enter the Union. As soon as the Annexation Bill was passed by the United States Congress, Don Juan Almonte, formerly aide-de-camp to General Santa Anna, now the Mexican minister at Washington, D.C., was recalled, and preparations for war were begun on a grand scale in Mexico.

In the meantime, the United States government had sent

[1] Anson Jones died at the Old Capital Hotel in Houston on the 7th of January, 1858. A short time before his death he remarked to one of his friends: "Here in this house, twenty years ago, I commenced my public career in Texas, and here I would like to die."

General Zachary Taylor to Corpus Christi on the Texas coast, with four thousand troops. He was ordered to march westward and take up a position on the Rio Grande River, the boundary line between Texas and Mexico. He was further ordered to confine himself to Texas soil unless the Mexicans should attempt to cross the river.

In the spring of 1846 General Taylor began his march across the country, "which appeared like one vast garden wavy with flowers of the most gorgeous dyes."[1] Then came a desert-like waste in which there was neither water nor any growing thing. "The sand was like hot ashes, and when you stepped upon it, you sank up to the ankles."[1]

But the region beyond the desert was fertile and inviting. At the Sal Colorado, a stream thirty miles east of the Rio Grande, some Mexican soldiers appeared. They insisted that all the country west of the Colorado belonged to Mexico, and declared that if the Americans attempted to cross that stream they would fire upon them. General Taylor paid no attention whatever to their threats. He led his troops over the Sal Colorado without further trouble and continued his march toward the Rio Grande.

There the war began in real earnest. The first battle was fought at Fort Brown (now Brownsville), opposite Matamoras. The Americans were victorious. Two other successful engagements, Palo Alto and Resaca de la Palma, took place on Texas territory. Then General Taylor, having received large reinforcements, entered Mexico and marched upon Monterey, the great interior city of northern Mexico.

About this time Santa Anna, who had been in exile and disgrace, returned to Mexico, and was immediately made commander-in-chief of the Mexican army.

Texas furnished her share of men for the war upon her hereditary foe. Governor Henderson himself entered the

---

[1] Diary of Captain Henry, U. S. A.

campaign as a major-general of volunteers; ex-President Lamar and Edward Burleson served upon his staff. Albert Sidney Johnston commanded a regiment. "Jack" Hays and George T. Wood, afterward governor of Texas, were also in command of regiments. Ben McCulloch carried into the war a company of rangers.

The Texans were in the van in every battle. At the storming of Monterey they especially distinguished themselves by their daring and high courage. A participator in the siege of the city says: "In order to dislodge the skirmishers from the housetops, the Texans rushed from door to door, breaking through buildings and inside walls; and, mounting to a level with the enemy, picked them off with their rifles. Meanwhile those in the streets charged from square to square amid sweeping showers of grape, cheered on by Lamar, Henderson, and Jefferson Davis of the Mississippi regiment." The next day "the artillery on both sides raked the streets, the balls striking the houses with a terrible crash, while amid the roar of cannon was heard the battering instruments of the Texans. Doors were forced open, walls were battered down, entrances were made through stone and brick, and the enemy were driven from point to point, followed by the sharp crack of the Texan rifles."

General Ampudia, who had so basely betrayed the trust of the Texans after their surrender at Mier in 1843, was in command of the Mexican forces. After three days of desperate fighting he surrendered the city of Monterey to General Taylor.

The officers commissioned by Taylor to draw up the articles of capitulation on the American side were Generals Worth and Henderson (governor of Texas) and Colonel Jefferson Davis.

Texas furnished above eight thousand soldiers for this war, and the "murderous ring of the Texan rifle" was heard on almost every field.

In New Mexico, where there was considerable fighting, the

cannon taken from General McLeod in the fatal Santa Fé expedition in 1841 was discovered by the American soldiers, where it had been hidden in the mountains. "It is," says the record, "a six-pounder, bearing the 'Lone Star' of Texas and the name of her ex-President, Mirabeau B. Lamar." The Americans adopted it as a favorite, and used it in firing their morning and evening signals. The Lone Star, they declared, brought them good luck.

The war ended in the storming and capture of the city of Mexico by General Winfield Scott, commander-in-chief of the United States army. Santa Anna, once more defeated and humbled, hid himself with the remains of his army in the mountain passes of Mexico.

Benjamin McCulloch.

In one of the last battles of the war Colonel Samuel H. Walker was killed. This dashing young Texan had been again and again selected by General Taylor for dangerous service, and his gallantry was a by-word in the army. He had been one of the unfortunate Mier prisoners, and was among those who overpowered the guard at Salado and escaped, only to be recaptured. In the death-lottery he had drawn a white bean, and had afterward endured the miseries of the Castle of Perote. In the neighborhood of that prison he fell mortally wounded, but flushed with victory, and soon afterward expired. "Few men were more lamented. When the cry 'Walker is dead' rang through the company, the hardy soldiers burst into tears."[1]

[1] Frost's *History of Mexico*.

Mexico signed at Guadalupe, Hidalgo, a treaty with the United States (February 2, 1848), and abandoned forever all claim to Texas.

The governors who succeeded Henderson in Texas from 1847 to 1859 were Governors George T. Wood, Hansborough P. Bell, Elisha M. Pease, and Hardin R. Runnels.

Early in Governor Wood's administration a disagreement arose between Texas and the United States over Sante Fé and the surrounding country. This had been a part of Texas, but was ceded in 1848 by Mexico to the United States with New Mexico. When the United States took possession of it Texas protested, and much ill-feeling followed. For a time it seemed, as if the state which had just got into the Union would march out again.

But the question was settled during Governor Bell's term of office. The disputed territory was bought by the United States from Texas for the sum of ten million dollars.

During these years Texas grew in prosperity; all boundary questions were settled, and the public debt was paid. Settlements sprung up to the very border. This, however, caused fresh trouble among the Indians, who from time to time fell upon isolated settlements, burning the houses and killing the settlers or carrying them into captivity. As late as 1847 two hundred Lipans on the war-path swept the western frontier. In 1848 the Indians in Texas killed one hundred and seventy persons, carried twenty-five into captivity, and stole six thousand horses.

The Texan rangers were ordered out by Governor Wood to protect the frontier. The Comanches, the fiercest of the western tribes, were finally defeated by the rangers under Colonel John S. Ford. Their chief, Iron Jacket, was killed in a desperate hand-to-hand combat with Captain S. P. Ross. The chief's tall form was found, after death, to be encased in a fine coat of scale armor, supposed to have belonged to some Spaniard in the days of the conquest of Mexico. Hence his name, Iron Jacket, and the belief that he could not be killed by the bullet of the white man. Iron Jacket's little son Noh-po was carried to Waco, where he was raised by the Ross family. During the administration of Governor Pease, the legislature gave the Indians twelve leagues of land and built for them several new trading-posts along the frontier. Later they were all removed to the Indian Territory.

Two million dollars were set aside by the state for a permanent school fund; and a quantity of land was voted for the support of the deaf and dumb, the blind, the orphan, and the insane.

A new state capitol, a Land Office, and other public buildings were erected at Austin.

In 1857 there was an uprising of Texan wagoners against the Mexican cartmen, who were engaged in hauling goods from the coast towns to San Antonio. Mexican labor was much cheaper than any other, and a large number of these teamsters, who were honest and reliable, were employed by merchants and planters. The Texan wagoners, failing to drive out Mexican cartmen by threats, raided them on the roads, drove off their oxen, broke up their carts, and in some instances killed the drivers.

Governor Pease, by ordering out a company of rangers to protect the Mexican teamsters, finally put a stop to the "Cart War," as it was called.

No other trouble marred this bright period. "Our inhabitants," said Governor Pease, in his message to the legislature in 1855, "are prosperous and happy to a degree unexampled in our former history."

3. DYING RACES.

The Indian tribes who possessed the fair land of Texas when the white man first set foot on its soil were rapidly dying out. Some were already extinct, having left hardly a trace to show where their villages and wigwams had once stood. The Cenis, that noble nation which welcomed La Salle and nursed him tenderly when he lay for months "sick of a fever" in their midst, and who sheltered the fleeing fugitives from Fort St. Louis, — these had entirely passed away. So had the kindly Coushattis, the friends of Lallemand's colonists; and the Orquisacas, the Nacogdoches, and all those gentler tribes by whose help the Franciscan friars had built the earliest missions. Gone were the music-loving Wacoes from the banks of the Brazos; and from the Trinity the corn-growing Tehas.

The fierce Carankawaes, once the terror of the coast and long believed to be cannibals, and the Kiowas, called the *red-eyed*, had melted before the coming of the pale-faces, as the snow melts under the April sun.

But remnants of the warlike western tribes remained. The Comanches, the Apaches, and the Lipans still hovered like dark clouds about the frontier. They called themselves *Nianis* (live Indians); and though they were taken away by the government from their hunting-grounds and penned up in a Reservation (that is, upon lands reserved or set apart for them), they continued every now and then to swoop down upon their old haunts, where every rock and bush and hillock was familiar to them. Even within the past twenty years the borderman dared not be too far from his rifle.

But the Texas Indian was passing. His tribes were dying out, as the Mohicans, the Powhatans, and the Alabamas had died out before them.

With the Red Man, another race, as wild, as noble, and as free as his, was as slowly drifting to its end.

When La Salle sailed up a certain pleasant stream in 1685, he called it *Les Vaches* (the cows), from the number of buffalos grazing on its banks. They roamed the vast prairies and the shaded timberland, from the utmost verge of the country on the north and west to the salt waters of the Gulf. The herds were so large that the thunder of their hoofs startled the air and their trampling shook the ground.

As the Indian retreated westward, the shaggy buffalo followed his moccasined foot ; as the savage warriors, who were as the sands of the seashore for numbers, dwindled away, so dwindled the buffalo herds.

4. THE TEXAS RANGER.

The daring and ever-watchful foe of the Texas Indian, the dashing and ever-ready hunter of the Texas buffalo, was the Texas ranger. He, too, is passing away before the march of civilization, and fast becoming a memory only ; but a memory which will live forever in song and story, with the brave, the generous, and the noble of all times.

The first company of Texas rangers was formed in 1832 ; but it was not until the administration of President Burnet (1836) that this arm of the service was regularly organized and put into the field.

They became at once a power, and they have since played an important part in the history of the state. Mounted upon a swift horse, with a *lariat* (rope) coiled about the high pommel of his saddle and a blanket strapped behind him ; with his long rifle resting in the hollow of his arm, and the bridle held loosely in his hand ; erect and graceful, the brim of his slouch hat hiding the sparkle of his keen eyes, — the Texas ranger is a striking and picturesque figure. But he is more than that. For fifty years and more he has been the terror of

Indian and intruding Mexican, of thief and desperado, of lawlessness and crime.

The rangers are subject to the call of the government. "But no tap of spirit-stirring drum or piercing fife, no trumpet call or bugle sound was heard on the border," in those early days. A rider passed from settlement to settlement, from home to home; there would be wiping of rifles and moulding of bullets. Oftener than otherwise it was the wives and the sisters and the sweethearts who moulded the bullets and packed the wallets, while the men ground their knives and saddled their horses. Then with a hurried good-bye, the rangers were mounted and away; now on the bloody trail of the Comanches, now tracking the fierce Lipans; to-day protecting a lonely frontier cabin, to-morrow helping the Mexican teamsters in the cart war.

A Texas Ranger.

The rangers, during the war of the United States with Mexico, were noted for their courage and gallantry. "I have seen a goodly number of volunteers in my day," a war correspondent wrote of them at that time, "but the Texas rangers are choice specimens. From the time we left Matamoras until we reached this place (Reynoso), the men never took off their coats, boots, or spurs. And although the weather was rainy and two fierce northers visited us, there was not a minute when any man's rifle or pistol would have missed fire or he could not have been up and ready for an attack."[1]

Another writer describes the rangers in camp: "Men in groups, with long beards and mustachios, were occupied in drying their blankets and cleaning and firing their guns. Some were cooking at the camp-fires, others were grooming their horses. They all wore belts of pistols around their waists and slouched hats, the uniform of the Texas ranger. They were a rough-looking set; but among them were doctors, lawyers, and many a college graduate. While standing in their midst I saw a young fellow come into the camp with a rifle on his shoulder and a couple of ducks in his hand. He addressed the captain: "Ben," he said, "if you haven't had dinner, you'd better mess with me, for I know none of the rest have fresh grub to-day."

The "captain" was Benjamin McCulloch, famous in the annals of the rangers. He is thus described by Samuel Reid, one of his own men:

"Captain McCulloch is a man of rather delicate frame, about five feet ten inches in height, with light hair and complexion. His features are regular and pleasing, though from long exposure on the frontier they have a weatherbeaten cast. His quick, bright blue eyes and thin compressed lips indicate the cool and calculating, as well as the brave and daring, energy of the man."

McCulloch was a Tennesseean by birth. His father served under General Jackson during the Creek war. Ben followed the trade of a hunter until he was twenty-one years old. In those days the settlers depended chiefly on bear meat for food. If a man were a poor marksman he sometimes went without his breakfast. But young McCulloch was a fine shot; he often killed as many as eighty bears in the course of a season.

He came to Texas with David Crockett. A fortunate illness

[1] G. W. Kendall.

kept him at Nacogdoches until after the fall of the Alamo, where Crockett perished. He served in the artillery at the battle of San Jacinto, and was one of the first to join the "ranging service." He was in almost all the expeditions of his time, and engaged in nearly all the fights.

The most noted ranger of this period, however, was Colonel John Coffin Hays, familiarly known as "Jack" Hays. Samuel Reid says of him:

John Coffin Hays.

"I had heard so much of Colonel Hays that I was anxious to meet the commander of our regiment. On this occasion I saw a group of gentlemen sitting around a camp-fire. Among them were General Mirabeau Lamar, Governor Henderson, and General McLeod, all distinguished men of Texas whose names are enrolled on the page of history. As I cast my eyes around the group, I tried to single out the celebrated partisan chief; and I was much surprised to be introduced to a slender, delicate-looking young man who proved to be Colonel Jack Hays. He was dressed quite plainly, and wore the usual broad-brimmed Texas hat and a loose open collar, with a black handkerchief tied carelessly around his neck. He has dark brown hair and large, brilliant hazel eyes which are restless in conversation and speak a language of their own not to be mistaken. His forehead is broad and high. He looks thoughtful and careworn, though very boyish. His modesty is extreme."

Colonel Hays was also a Tennesseean. He emigrated to Texas when but nineteen years of age. His talent as a leader showed itself early; and at the age of twenty-one (1840) he was placed in command of the frontier, with the rank of major. He soon became famous as a fighter of the Indians, by whom he was both feared and admired. "Me and Blue Wing," said a Comanche chief on one occasion, "we no afraid to go anywhere *together*, but Captain Jack *great brave*. He no afraid to go anywhere *by himself*."

His regiment of rangers which included McCulloch's company was foremost in every battle of the war with Mexico. His word was law with his men. Off duty he was a gay and pleasant companion; the rangers called him Jack, but there was something about him which kept them from taking any liberties with him.

The rangers continued to serve the state after peace was made with Mexico. In 1862 the legislature passed a law for the protection of the frontier. This law provided for the raising of ten companies of rangers of one hundred men each. Each company was to be divided, and the two detachments stationed about one day's ride apart, just beyond the settlements.

The command of this regiment was given to Colonel J. H. Norris. He went at once to the frontier. He distributed his soldiers from the Red River to the Rio Grande, with orders for each company to send a scout every day from one station to the next, the scout to return the following day. This plan gave a patrol scout from Red River to the Rio Grande every day. In addition to this, each company kept out a flying scout all the time.

"This," remarks an old ranger (E. L. Denton), "was a busy year for both rangers and Indians."

On the 8th of January, 1864, five hundred rangers, under Captains Gillentine, Fossett, and Totten, met and defeated two thousand Comanche Indians on Dove Creek in what is now Tom Green County. This was one of the last pitched battles fought with Indians on Texas soil.

In later years the rangers have served as a sort of state police. Many a stronghold of cattle thieves has been raided by them; many a nest of desperadoes has been broken up; many a bitter neighborhood feud has been settled.

At the present time (1896) there are about two hundred rangers in the service. They furnish their own horses, and receive forty dollars a month; their rations and their arms being supplied by the state.

Some of those noted for steady nerve and daring courage among the ranger captains of earlier and later times are Colonel "Rip" Ford, Lawrence Sullivan Ross (since governor of Texas, and called by his old comrades "Sul" Ross), Colonel "Buck" Barry, Lieutenant Chrisman, Sergeants J. B. Armstrong and L. P. Selker, and Captains Tom Wright, Jesse Lee Hall, and L. B. McNulty.

5. A CLOUD IN THE SKY.

In the spring of 1848 there appeared on the streets of Austin a young man wearing a costume which attracted much attention. It was composed of gray stockings and knee breeches, with a black velvet tunic and broad-brimmed, gray felt hat. The rather dashing-looking stranger was evidently French, but he called himself an Icarian. He was, in fact, on his way from New Braunfels, where he had been living, to Icaria, a new settlement near the Cross Timbers in Fannin County.

This settlement was founded by Etienne Cabet (Ca-bā), a Frenchman who dreamed of establishing a community where nobody would be rich and nobody would be poor, but all money and other property would be held in common. Devotion to women and children, honesty, and the ability and willingness to work for the good of the brotherhood were the chief rules of the fraternity. They numbered in France in 1847 many thousand persons of all classes.

Cabet obtained from the Peters Immigration Company in 1847 a million acres of land in North Texas. The land was given to him on condition that a settlement should be made upon it before the 1st of July, 1848. In January, 1848, the first cohort, numbering sixty-nine persons, embarked at Havre, France. They arrived at Shreveport, Louisiana, the following April. From there they marched on foot to their chosen home in Texas, carrying firearms, household goods, and provisions.

"Oh, if you could see Icaria!" they presently wrote back to the brotherhood in France. "It is an Eden. The forests are superb; the vegetation rich and varied. We have horses, cows, pigs, and chickens in abundance. . . . Many Texans come to see us. They are good-natured and very honest. We camp and sleep out of doors. We lock up nothing and are never robbed."[1]

Houses were built and fields ploughed and planted. By midsummer the Icarians in their cosy hamlet were on the lookout for the second cohort of colonists. But before it arrived the cholera broke out in Icaria. Many of the settlers died; nearly all those who were left abandoned their homes in a panic and returned to New Orleans, where Cabet himself joined them with several hundred recruits from France. A new and more fortunate Icarian settlement was finally made in Missouri.

A few years later (1853) a procession, also composed of French emigrants, passed along Main Street in Houston. They had just landed from the steamboat *Eclipse* on the bayou at the foot of the street. At their head walked a tall gentleman in a velvet coat and three-cornered hat. He carried a drawn sword in his hand, and the tricolored flag of France floated above his head. His long white hair streamed over his shoulders. The whole company, men,

[1] *Cabet et ses Icariens.*

women, and children, sung the Marseillaise hymn as they marched along.

The tall gentleman was the Count Victor Considerant. He had come with his followers from France to Texas to found a Phalanstery, a community much like that already attempted by Cabet. His watchword was "Liberty and Equality." The faces of the emigrants lighted with joy as they traveled away over the prairies, following this beautiful vision.

They founded their town on the east fork of the Trinity River, in Dallas County, and called it Reunion. But the brotherhood soon fell to pieces. The emigrants scattered over the country, finding it pleasanter to own homes in a land of true liberty and equality, than to live by the count's fine theories.

Many descendants both of the Icarians and of Count Considerant's colonists are to be met with in North Texas.

Sam Houston succeeded Runnels as governor in 1859. When he took his seat at Austin, clouds from more than one quarter were gathering in the clear sky of Texas. Roving bands of Indians from the Territory came across the border and murdered in cold blood a number of families. At first they stole in, made their raids, and dashed back in a single night. But they grew more and more bold and insolent, until the governor was obliged to send the rangers to their old work of watching the frontier.

Lawrence Sullivan Ross, afterward governor of Texas, was at this time a lieutenant in the ranging service. He was a gallant and dashing soldier. During a raid on the Indians, on Pease River (1860), he rescued Cynthia Ann Parker, a white woman, who had been carried away by the Comanches, when but nine years of age. She had been a captive twenty-four years and had forgotten her native tongue. She was the wife of Peta Nocona, a Comanche chief, and the mother of several children. Lieutenant Ross returned her to her kindred with her little daughter Ta-ish-put (Prairie Flower). But she was not happy among these long-unknown white people; she pined for her dusky adopted kinsmen; and four years after her rescue she died, little Ta-ish-put soon following her to the Happy Hunting-grounds. Inanah Parker, one of her sons, became a Comanche chief.

During this period a Mexican bandit named Cortina crossed the lower Rio Grande into Texas at the head of four hundred men. Their object was plunder, and in their forays a great many innocent people were killed. The governor appealed to the general government at Washington for protection along the Mexican border.

The War Department in response ordered Colonel Robert E. Lee (afterward famous as commander-in-chief of the Confederate States army), then stationed at San Antonio, to attack the bandit and drive him out, crossing the Rio Grande, if necessary, in pursuit.

Some United States troops, with several companies of rangers, were at once put in the field, and Cortina's band was soon broken up.

These troubles were light, however, compared with those which were about to follow.

The two sections of the United States, the North and the South, had for some years been drifting apart. Their views differed widely on several important questions, particularly the question of states' rights, and there seemed to be no chance of a mutual agreement. In 1860, at the time Abraham Lincoln was elected President, the Southern States determined to withdraw from the Union. They believed that each state had a right to withdraw or secede from the Union whenever that Union became for any reason undesirable to it, as the individual members of a family may leave the paternal home if they wish to do so. But the Northern States did not agree to this. They believed that the Union should be preserved, and that the states should be held together — even by the power of the sword.

South Carolina was the first state to secede from the Union. Texas, on hearing of this news, was filled with excitement. Military companies were formed all over the state; the air was thick with the flutter of secession flags; the ground echoed the tramp of awkward squads drilling under the eyes of officers as awkward and inexperienced and enthusiastic as themselves.

Governor Houston, as well as some other patriotic and true-hearted Texans, was bitterly opposed to secession, but his voice was lost in the loud clamor of public feeling.

A convention was held in Austin in January, 1861. A declaration of secession was drawn up and submitted to the people (February 23). Texas by a large majority voted herself out of the Union, which she had entered fifteen years before.

There was wild rejoicing over the state. The capitol at Austin was brilliantly illuminated, bonfires were lighted, bells were rung, the Confederate flag was run up on all public buildings, and the work of mustering troops into the Confederate States army instantly began.

All state officials were required to take the oath of fealty to the new government. Governor Houston, true to his convictions, refused to do this.

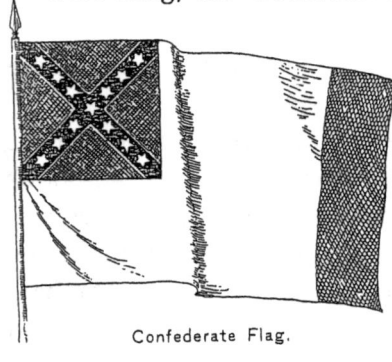

Confederate Flag.

When the day came for the ceremony (March 16), the hall of representatives was filled to overflowing. "The presiding officer, amid a profound silence, called three times: 'Sam Houston! Sam Houston! Sam Houston!'

but the governor remained in his office in the basement of the capitol whittling a pine stick, and hearing the echo of the noise and tumult above his head. Houston was declared deposed from his office, and Edward Clark, the lieutenant-governor, was installed as governor."[1]

Houston left Austin and retired to his place near Huntsville. To the end of his life he continued to declare that, although opposed to the war of the States, his sympathies were with Texas. "My state, right or wrong," he said. One of his sons entered the Confederate army with his consent and approval.

He died July 26, 1863, at the age of seventy years. His last words, whispered with dying lips, were: "Texas! Texas!"

And Texas, forgetting all her differences with him, and remembering only his ready and gallant services in her hours of need, mourned his loss as that of a well-beloved son.

[1] Williams' *Life of Houston*.

VIII.

GALVESTON.

(1861-1865.)

1. A BUFFALO HUNT.

The early months of the year 1861 in Texas were like one long holiday. The country was dotted with white tents where the recruits were encamped, and where, amid bursts of martial music and in all the glory of brand new uniforms, the untried volunteers received their mothers and sisters, and showed them with pride "how soldiers live in time of war."

Every few days one of these camps would be broken up, the tents and camp baggage would be loaded on wagons, and the "boys" would march to the nearest town. There the whole population would be gathered to greet them; a flag would be presented to them by the hand of some bright-eyed girl, loud cheers would echo on the air, and the company would tramp steadily away to take its place in the fighting ranks of the Confederate States army.

Many of these soldiers carried their negro body-servants with them; all had abundant stores of clothing and bedding, and of those little comforts and luxuries that only mothers know how to provide. Their young faces were eager, their eyes were sparkling, and if there were sobs in their throats as they said those last good-byes, the sobs were smothered in the ringing cheers which mingled with the notes of "Dixie" or "The Bonnie Blue Flag."

They were soon to learn in many a tentless camp, on many a foot-sore march, on many a bloody and hard-fought field, how soldiers really live in time of war.

But the days as yet were like one long holiday, although mother-hearts ached in secret dread, and the scarred veterans of the Texan revolution and of the Mexican War were filled with inward forebodings for the future.

People along the frontier had been talking for some time about a great buffalo hunt which was to take place that winter in the Pan Handle. John R. Baylor, a noted hunter and scout, had, it was said, raised more than a thousand men to go on this hunt, and a great many scouts and Indian fighters had joined him. Among them was Ben McCulloch, who had done such gallant service in Mexico under General Taylor.

The buffalo hunt did not take place; but Colonel Ben McCulloch, with the buffalo hunters, a thousand or more strong, appeared in San Antonio on the 15th of February (1861).

General David E. Twiggs, United States army, was at that time in command of the troops in Texas. San Antonio was the most important of the United States army posts in the southwest; a large amount of military stores was in the arsenal, and soldiers were kept there ready to march at need to the relief of the frontier forts.

Colonel McCulloch, acting under orders of commissioners from Austin, demanded the surrender of all military posts and supplies in the State of Texas. General Twiggs on the 18th of February made a formal surrender of the department. The United States troops were paroled and marched to Indianola on the coast, where the *Star of the West*, an unarmed United States steamer, was waiting to take them home.

But when they reached Indianola (18th of April) the *Star of the West* and the gunboat *Mohawk*, which had been guarding her, had both disappeared. The officer in command was in a quandary. He did not know what to do. At length he placed his troops on two schooners and sailed across the Matagorda Bay to the Gulf.

In the meantime, on the 12th of April, at Fort Sumter, South Carolina, the first gun of the Civil War had been fired. The struggle between the States had begun.

General Earl Van Dorn, of the Confederate army, was at this time in command of the military department of Texas. His headquarters were at Galveston. The island which the pirate Lafitte had left lone and deserted when he sailed away in the *Pride* now teemed with a busy and prosperous people. The huts of Campeachy were replaced by stately mansions, and beautiful gardens bloomed where sandy wastes had been.

Several companies of soldiers were encamped without the city, awaiting marching orders. General Van Dorn entered the camp one day, and after a brief speech called for volunteers for an expedition which he was about to undertake. The Galveston Artillery, the Island City Rifles, and an Irish company called the Wigfall Guards, at once stepped forward, eager for duty.

The next night (17th of April), about midnight, the steamboat *General Rusk*, with these volunteers on board, drew up alongside the *Star of the West*, lying in the Gulf of Mexico, off Indianola. Captain Howe, of the United States steamer, hearing himself hailed, came on deck, and supposing these to be the United States troops he was expecting, he politely ordered the *General Rusk* to be made fast to his own boat. In a twinkling the Confederate soldiers were aboard of the *Star of the West* demanding its surrender.

"To what flag am I asked to surrender?" asked the astonished captain. Ensign Duggan of the Wigfall Guards displayed the Lone Star flag of Texas, and in his richest brogue exclaimed: "That's it! Look at it, me byes. Did ye iver see the Texas flag on an Irish jackstaff before?"[1]

[1] Scharf's *History of the Confederate States Navy*.

Captain Howe, having neither arms nor soldiers, surrendered, and the *Star of the West* followed the *General Rusk* to Galveston.

This was why the United States troops the next morning (April 18) found no steamer to carry them away. The two schooners upon which they embarked were also captured several days later, having on board eight hundred officers and men, with three hundred fine rifles and a large quantity of camp supplies.

But the Confederacy had no means of protecting the long stretch of Texas coast. In July a blockading squadron — that is, a fleet of armed vessels to prevent ships from entering or leaving the harbor — was stationed in the Gulf off Galveston, and in a short time the whole coast was closely guarded.

In the fall of 1861 Frank R. Lubbock, who has been called the "war governor" of Texas, was elected governor. By the close of his term ninety thousand Texan soldiers were in the Confederate army.

Early in 1862 a Texas brigade, under General Sibley, was defeated by the Union forces in New Mexico, and forced to retreat to San Antonio with a loss of five hundred men.

In October of the same year the Confederates, unable to hold Galveston, surrendered that place to Commodore Eagle of the blockading squadron, and withdrew to Virginia Point on the mainland about six miles distant. Many of the citizens of the town also left their homes; and amid a silence almost as profound as that in which Lafitte landed on the island nearly fifty years before, several hundred soldiers stepped ashore from their boats and took possession of the place. The United States flag was hoisted on the Custom-house; the soldiers settled into their quarters on one of the wharves; the imposing vessels of the Federal squadron filled the bay and the harbor. A mournful cry echoed throughout Texas: "Galveston has fallen!"

2. THE BLUE AND THE GRAY.

The holiday look had long since disappeared from Texas. No battles had been fought within her borders, but the blood of her brave sons had dyed the sod of many a battlefield elsewhere. For the deadly conflict was raging. The North and the South, fighting as brother against brother, were pouring out their kindred blood day by day; the smoke of their hostile guns darkened the very heavens. Many heroic deeds were done on both sides — deeds which to-day thrill us with wonder and admiration.

But there were frightful gaps in the ranks of those who had marched away from Texas to the tune of "Dixie" or "The Bonnie Blue Flag." The gallant lads who had showed off their brave uniforms in the holiday camps were tramping about, barefoot, ragged, and hungry, in Virginia, in Tennessee, in Georgia, — wherever there was an enemy to be attacked or an outpost to be held.

Their mothers and sisters at home were making lint and cartridges, weaving and wearing homespun, making their own shoes and gloves, and cheering the far-away "boys" with letters and with home-made gifts, and praying, praying always.

There were few able-bodied men left in the state. The women with the old men and boys, aided by the negroes who remained loyal and trustworthy, made the crops. As the war went on the prices of everything rose. Old bills show that forty dollars a yard (Confederate money) was paid for calico for a little girl's "best" dress; and seventy-five dollars was paid for a boy's first pair of boots. A war-time arithmetic has among its examples the following:

"A cavalryman paid 200 dollars for his pistol and 4000 dollars for his horse; how much did both cost him?"

"At 20 dollars a pound, how much coffee can you buy for 40 dollars?"

"If one hat costs 120 dollars, how much would eight hats cost?"

Coffee and tea were replaced by drinks made of parched potatoes, or burnt peas, and sassafras roots. The real articles which were brought into the country occasionally by blockade-runners were known as "blockade" coffee and tea, and were kept for the use of the sick.

The blockade-runners were very daring and confident. Captain Henry Sherffius of Houston, among others, was noted for his skill in slipping through the line of big ships on watch along the coast of Texas. Once, when he was leaving on one of his trips, he was so sure of himself and his boat that he invited his friends to come to his wedding on a certain day some weeks later. He came back at the appointed time, bringing with him his wedding-cakes, baked in Vera Cruz, Mexico.

The Mississippi River rolled, a wide barrier, between the two parts of the Confederacy. Its banks were lined with Federal sharp-shooters, and its yellow waters were dotted with Federal gunboats. It was difficult to get news from the eastern side, where the greater part of the fighting was done, and terrible were the times of waiting between the first rumors of a battle and the receipt of the lists of the killed and wounded. A noble and patriotic citizen of Houston, E. H. Cushing, rendered a priceless service to Texas in this matter. He was at that time and had been for years the editor of the *Houston Telegraph*. His energy and his devotion to the Confederate cause were unceasing. He established a pony express between the seat of war — wherever that chanced to be — and Texas. His messengers somehow managed to get through the lines when no one else could do so. They went and came, carrying and bringing papers and dispatches, and above all, precious letters from the boys in gray. Mr. Cushing's express also "ran" to Brownsville.

At the close of the war this true patriot supplied money from his private purse, not only to broken-down and crippled home-coming Confederate soldiers, but to the home-going Federal prisoners from Camp Ford.[1]

The *Telegraph* came out daily throughout the war, some of its later numbers being printed on coarse yellow, red, and blue paper.

Amid all the anxiety and hardship there was no thought of giving up. The men of the South believed themselves to be fighting for a just cause; the Northern soldiers were equally sincere in their convictions. And so the war, grim and terrible, went on.

In the fall of 1862 General Magruder, Confederate States army, assumed command of the Trans-Mississippi (that is, west of the Mississippi) Department. He determined at once to attempt the recapture of Galveston. He went to Virginia Point, where the Confederate troops were camped, and there with great caution and secrecy made his plans.

At the head of Galveston Bay, the *Neptune* and the *Bayou City*, two small steamboats, were bulwarked with cotton bales, mounted with cannon, and manned with sharp-shooters from the Confederate States cavalry and artillery. The *Lady Gwinn* and the *John F. Carr* were detailed to accompany these vessels as tenders. This crude fleet was commanded by Captain Leon Smith who had served in the navy of the Texas Republic.

About midnight on the 31st of December, the boats moved down the bay to a position above the town, where they quietly awaited General Magruder's signal gun.

Magruder had already crossed his troops to the island. They marched swiftly through the deserted streets of the city, and, by the light of a waning moon, planted their batteries. At five o'clock on New Year's morning, 1863, the attack began. It was a complete surprise to the Federals.

---

[1] Camp Ford, where the Federal prisoners were confined during the war, was situated near Tyler, in Smith County.

The ships of the blockading fleet, under the command of Commodore Renshaw, were nearly all within the bay. The *Harriet Lane*, commanded by Commodore Wainwright, was lying near the wharf. At a little distance was the iron-clad *Westfield*, Commodore Renshaw's flag-ship, attended by the *Owasco;* still further out were the armed vessels, the *Clifton* and the *Sachem*, and the barges the *Elias Park* and the *Cavallo*.

The war-ships answered the fire of Magruder's batteries with a terrific hail of iron; once the Confederate gunners were driven from their guns. But the *Neptune* and the *Bayou City* steamed up to the *Harriet Lane* and attacked her at close quarters, pouring a hot fire into her from behind the rampart of cotton bales.

The *Neptune* with a hole in her hull made by a cannon-ball soon sank in shallow water. The *Bayou City* was also disabled. The Confederate sharp-shooters leaped on board the *Harriet Lane*, and, after a bloody fight on her deck, captured her.[1] Commodore Wainwright was killed early in the action. First Lieutenant Lea was mortally wounded.

The Union infantry made a gallant resistance to the land attack, but they were finally obliged to surrender.

The *Sachem*, the *Clifton*, and the *Owasco* stood out to sea and escaped. The *Westfield* ran aground and was blown up to prevent her capture. Commodore Renshaw and his officers had left the vessel, but their boats were too near when the explosion took place prematurely, and they perished with her. The *Harriet Lane* and the barges, with several hundred prisoners, remained in the hands of the victors.

The loss in this battle on the Confederate side was twelve killed and seventy wounded. The Federals lost one hundred and fifty killed and many wounded.

Among the mortally wounded were two young soldiers, the

---

[1] The bell used on the *Harriet Lane* is now in the museum of the Houston (Texas) High School.

story of whose death even yet stirs the heart to pity. One fell fighting under the starry cross of the Confederacy. The other dropped on the bloody deck of the *Harriet Lane* under the shadow of the stars and stripes. The Confederate was Lieutenant Sidney Sherman, son of the gallant veteran, General Sidney Sherman, who led the infantry charge at San Jacinto. The lieutenant was hardly more than a boy. The blood oozed from his wounds as he lay dying, but the smile of victory parted his lips. Suddenly his blue eyes grew soft and tender "Break this gently to my mother," he whispered. These were his last words.

The young Union soldier was Edward Lea, first lieutenant of the *Harriet Lane*. His wounds were also fatal. But as his life was ebbing away he heard his name spoken in a tone of agony. He opened his eyes. His father, Major Lea of the Confederate army, was kneeling beside him. Father and son had fought on opposite sides that dark New Year's morning. The pale face of the young lieutenant lighted with joy; and when a little later the surgeon told him he had but a moment to live, he answered with the confidence of a little child and with his latest breath, "My father is here."

The two lads cold in death rested almost side by side on their funeral biers that day, — brothers in death, brothers for ever in the memory of those who looked upon their calm young faces.

Lieutenant Lea and Commodore Wainwright were buried with military honors from General Magruder's headquarters, Major Lea reading the service for the burial of the dead.

The body of young Sherman was carried to his beloved mother, who in her home on the bay had listened with a beating heart to the cannonading of the battle in which her son's brave young life had ended.

3. HOME AGAIN.

A small earthwork called Fort Griffin had been built by the Confederates on the Texas side of Sabine Pass at the mouth of the Sabine River. It was protected by five light guns and garrisoned by the Davis Guards, a company from Houston commanded by Captain Odlum. The first lieutenant of the company was Dick Dowling, an Irishman but twenty years of age.

Fort Griffin, though small, was a place of much importance. Sabine Pass was a sort of outlet for the pent-up Confederacy. Blockade-runners, in spite of the Federal ships stationed in the Gulf, were always slipping out of the Sabine River, loaded with cotton for Cuba or Europe, and stealing in with arms and supplies from Mexico.

Richard Dowling.

Soon after the battle of Galveston, Major Oscar Watkins, Confederate States navy, was sent by General Magruder with two cotton-clad steamboats, the *Josiah Bell* and the *Uncle Ben*, to annoy the blockading fleet at Sabine Pass. After a skirmish and an exciting chase, he succeeded in capturing two United States ships, the *Velocity* and the *Morning Light* (January 21, 1863).

The United States then determined to take Fort Griffin and land at Sabine Pass a force large enough to overawe that part of the country. Twenty-two transports carried the land troops, about fifteen thousand in number, to the Pass. Four gunboats, the *Sachem*, the *Clifton*, the *Arizona*, and the *Granite City*, accompanied them, to bombard the fort and cover the landing of the soldiers. The expedition was under the command of General Franklin.

When this formidable fleet appeared at Sabine Pass, Captain Odlum was absent and Lieutenant Dowling was in command of Fort Griffin. His whole force consisted of forty-two men. He ordered the "Davys," as they were called, to stay in the bomb-proofs until he himself should fire the first gun. Then, hidden by the earthwork, he watched the approach of the gunboats.

The *Clifton* steamed in and opened the attack from her pivot gun, throwing a number of shells which dropped into the fort and exploded. The *Sachem* and the *Arizona* followed, pouring in broadsides from their thirty-two-pound cannon.

No reply came from the fort, which seemed to be deserted. The gunboats came nearer and nearer. Suddenly a shot from the fort clove the air and fell hissing into the water beyond the *Arizona*. The fight at once became furious. The *Clifton* and the *Arizona* moved backward and forward, vomiting huge shells which tore the earthwork of the fort and filled the air with dust. Ships and fort seemed wrapped in flame. The *Sachem* meanwhile was stealing into the Pass toward the unprotected rear of the fort. But a well-aimed shot from Dowling's battery struck her, crushing her iron plating and causing her to rise on end and quiver like a leaf in the wind. She was at the mercy of the fort, and her flag was instantly lowered. The *Clifton* kept up the fight with great skill and bravery. But she soon ran aground in the shallows, where she continued to fire until a shot passed through her boiler, completely wrecking her. A white flag was run up at her bow, and the battle was over. The *Arizona* and the *Granite City* steamed out to the transports, whose men had watched the fight with breathless interest.

The fleet at once retired, leaving the *Sachem* and the *Clifton* to the "Davys."[1]

Three hundred Union soldiers were taken prisoners. Captain Crocker of the *Clifton* came ashore with a boat's crew, and, mounting the parapet, asked for the commanding officer. Lieutenant Dowling, covered with the dust of the fort, presented himself as the person sought.

The gallant Federal in his handsome uniform could hardly believe that this dirty little boy was his conqueror, or that the handful of men before him comprised the force which had so calmly awaited a hostile fleet and defeated it.[2]

Eight months afterward the United States gunboats, the *Granite City* and the *Wave*, were captured at Sabine Pass.

In November and December, 1863, General Banks took possession of the Texas coast, protecting it with a land force from Brownsville to Indianola. Within a short time, however, he withdrew his troops, leaving only a garrison at Brownsville. But the cruel war was fast drawing to a close. The Confederate army, thinned in ranks and in need of food, as well as of powder and of shot, could no longer be maintained. There were no men to take the place of those who fell in battle; the untilled fields gave no harvests; the coasts were so guarded that the most reckless blockade-runner, could no longer get in with supplies. On the 9th of April, 1865, General Robert E. Lee, commander-in-chief of the Confederate army, surrendered to General U. S. Grant at Appomattox Court House in Virginia.

Before this news reached Texas the last skirmish of the war had taken place near Brownsville (April 13) between some

---

[1] Jefferson Davis, in his *Rise and Fall of the Confederate Government*, says of this engagement: "The success of the single company which garrisoned the earthwork at Fort Griffin is without parallel in ancient or modern war."

[2] Scharf's *History of the Confederate States Navy*.

of Banks' soldiers and a party of Confederates. The scene of this skirmish was the old battlefield of Palo Alto.

On the 30th of May Generals Kirby Smith and Magruder went on board the United States ship *Fort Jackson* at Galveston and made a formal surrender of the Trans-Mississippi Department.

On the 19th of June General Granger, United States army, took command at the island and announced the freedom of the negroes.

The great Civil War was over.

Several thousand Texans lost their lives in the Confederate States army during the four years' war. Among the distinguished dead were General John Gregg, first general of Hood's brigade, Colonels Tom Lubbock and Tom Green, the famous scout Ben McCulloch, General Granbury, Colonel Rogers, and many others. To these may be added General Albert Sidney Johnston, always claimed by Texas as her son, and who in death rests upon her bosom.

The war was over. The ragged, foot-sore, hungry soldiers who had so proudly worn the gray began to come home. Many who had gone away round-faced boys came back lank and hollow-eyed men. Many were maimed and crippled; many were sick; all were forlorn and discouraged. They saw with despair their weed-grown fields, their dilapidated houses, and rotting fences. The wives and mothers, whose husbands and sons had laid down their lives for a lost cause, looked at the more fortunate wives and mothers whose husbands and sons had been spared to them, and wept. And all wondered how they could ever take up their ruined lives again.

But time is merciful. The gloom did not last always. The Blue and the Gray clasped hands before many years had passed, and once more the Lone Star of Texas blazed in a cloudless sky.

IX.

THIRTY YEARS.

(1865-1895.)

THE time indeed came when the Blue and the Gray joined hands, and the Lone Star shone once more in a cloudless sky. But that time was not yet. The years which followed the Civil War were bitter and sorrowful ones for Texas.

After the surrender General Granger continued to hold military possession of the state.

Before his arrival Pendleton Murrah, who had succeeded Lubbock in 1863, had left his office in the hands of the lieutenant-governor Fletcher S. Stockdale, and gone to Mexico.

Andrew J. Hamilton was appointed provisional governor by President Johnson. He arrived at Galveston in July (1865), and at once assumed the duties of his office.

He ordered an election of delegates to a convention which was called for the purpose of framing a new constitution.

But no man was allowed to vote who had borne arms against the United States. The majority of Texas men had fought against the Union; they therefore took little interest in an election of delegates for whom they could not vote.

The convention met (February, 1866), the new constitution was drawn up and submitted for ratification to such of the people as were "loyal to the United States, and none others"; and in June James W. Throckmorton was elected governor.

A few months later the United States government decided to place the state again under military rule. Louisiana and Texas were constituted a Military District with headquarters at New Orleans. General Philip Sheridan was placed in command, and General Charles Griffin was ordered to Texas with several thousand troops to enforce military rule (March, 1867). His headquarters were at Galveston.

All elections except those under control of his officers were forbidden by General Griffin. An oath, known as the "iron-clad oath," was required of all voters. The newly freed negroes were for the first time placed on juries and encouraged to vote.

It was during this time that the remains of the great soldier General Albert Sidney Johnston were removed from New Orleans to Austin for final burial.

At Houston, when the funeral train rolled into the station, it was met by a procession of five hundred ladies and little girls. The coffin was borne to the old Houston Academy, where for a day and night it lay in state, amid the mournful tolling of bells.

General Albert Sidney Johnston.

In July Governor Throckmorton, upon reports made by General Griffin, was removed from office by General Sheridan, and E. M. Pease appointed in his place.

In September, 1869, Governor Pease, vexed and wearied by the strife and discord around him, resigned his thankless office. For a time there was no governor, a military adjutant performing the duties of the place.

In 1870 Edmund J. Davis was inaugurated governor and held the office four years. He was succeeded in 1874 by Richard Coke, with Richard B. Hubbard as lieutenant-governor.

The dark and stormy period from the surrender to the close of Governor Davis' term of office has since been known in Texas as the " Reconstruction Time."

At the time of Governor Davis' election, the military was finally withdrawn from the state, the citizens were restored to their civil rights, and Texas was readmitted to the Union. During his administration a Homestead Law was passed, a one-per-cent tax was levied for the building of schoolhouses, and the growth of railroads was encouraged by liberal grants of land.

But there was still a great deal of trouble and discontent, and it was not until Governor Coke took his seat that the state, so long shaken by contention, began once more to breathe freely and to put forth the strength within her.

Governor Coke served from 1874 to 1876; in 1876 he was elected to the United States senate, and Richard B. Hubbard became governor (1876–1879).

The governors who guided the Ship of State from 1879 to 1895 were Oran M. Roberts (1879–1883), John Ireland[1] (1883–1887), Lawrence S. Ross (1887–1891), and James S. Hogg (1891–1895).

In 1894 Charles A. Culberson was elected governor. He was inaugurated in 1895.

These years have been marked by many wonderful changes in Texas. Not the least of these changes has been the growth of the great public school system. The first free school in Texas was opened at San Antonio in 1844. A state public school system was organized in 1870. From these imperfect beginnings to the admirable system of to-day, when an army of earnest and gifted men and women are banded together in the noble work of teaching, and countless multitudes of children

---

[1] Ireland died March 15, 1896.

pass daily in and out of the schoolroom, — from that gray dawn to this blazing noontide, what a change!

The cause of education has indeed been ever in the minds and hearts of the people.

An Agricultural and Mechanical College was founded at Bryan, and opened in 1876.

In 1879 a State Normal School for teachers, called the

The Sam Houston Normal Institute.

Sam Houston Normal Institute, was established at Huntsville, Governor Houston's old home. A few years later the Prairie View, a normal school for colored teachers, was established.

A State University was founded in 1881. The fine group of buildings crowning one of Austin's green hills was finished and thrown open to the young men and women students of the state in 1883.

The first president of the University Board of Regents was Doctor Ashbel Smith. After his services to the Texan Republic, Doctor Smith devoted himself to scientific study and to the free practice of the medical profession. In 1861 he enlisted in the Confederate States army. He was elected a captain in the second Texas regiment of infantry, and was promoted to the colonelcy on the battlefield of Shiloh for personal bravery. He was in command of the post of Galveston at the time of the final surrender. He was chairman of the committee sent

The University of Texas.

from Galveston to New Orleans to escort to Texas the remains of General Albert Sidney Johnston.

His wise counsels were of great service during those troublous times. The joy and pride of this truly great man's declining years was the University of Texas. He lived to see it answer to his highest hopes ; and his memory should be eternally associated with its fame.

A number of charitable and other public institutions have been added to those already in existence. The new Penitentiary at Rusk (1877), a State Orphan's Asylum at Corsicana (1881), and two Insane Asylums, one at Terrell (1883) and one at San Antonio (1890), are among these. In 1891 the John B. Hood Camp of Confederate Veterans at Austin was taken under the kindly care of the state, and its name changed to the Texas Confederate Home.

Many state questions of importance have been considered; new laws have been made and old ones improved.

The public debt has been reduced. A new constitution has been adopted by the people (1875).

In 1895 suit was brought by Texas, in the Supreme Court of the United States, for Greer County, a body of land on Red River claimed both by the United States government and Texas. The decision of the Supreme Court (April, 1896) awarded the county to the United States.

The Old Alamo Monument.

A new court, called the Commission of Appeals, was created in 1881; the same year an admirable quarantine system was established, with a special station at Galveston.

A railroad commission was formed in 1891. In 1891, also, the United States government began at Galveston the building of jetties to improve the entrance to the harbor. These jetties, which are a double line of gigantic stone walls, reach out from the land into the Gulf. The action of the tides within this artificial channel washes out the sand, and thus deepens it. Jetties are also being built at Sabine Pass and at Aransas Pass.

In 1881 the old capitol at Austin was burned, and with it many priceless relics of the earlier days of Texas. Among these was the old monument dedicated in 1857 to the heroes of the Alamo. It was built of stones from the ruined fortress and stood on the porch of the capitol. It was inscribed with the names of Travis and his men; and the four sides of the shaft bore the following inscriptions:

North. "To the God of the fearless and the free is dedicated this altar, made from the stones of the Alamo."
West. "Blood of heroes hath stained me. Let the stones of the Alamo speak that their immolation be not forgotten."
South. "Be they enrolled with Leonidas in the host of the mighty dead."
East. "Thermopylæ had her messenger of defeat, but the Alamo had none."

A new monument, upon whose summit stands, rifle in hand, the statue of a Texas ranger, has been placed in the capitol grounds.

The legislature which met soon after the burning of the old capitol provided for the erection of a new one. Three million acres of public lands were set aside to meet this expense. The new building was finished and dedicated in 1888.

The historic old church of the Alamo was purchased by the state in 1883. It is earnestly hoped by all lovers of Texas history that the battlefield of San Jacinto, and other places made sacred by the blood of Texan heroes, may in the near future likewise become the property of the state.

X.

TEXAS.

FROM THE DOME OF THE CAPITOL.

On the 16th of May, 1888, there was a mighty gathering of people at Austin. They had come — men, women, and children — from every quarter of the great state: from the Pan Handle and from the coast; from the wide prairies of the west, and the wooded hills and valleys of the east. There was a throb of pride in every heart and a sparkle of joy in every eye; for Texas was about to give a housewarming, as it were, and her children had met together to have a share in the home feast, — the new capitol was to be dedicated.

The beautiful City of Hills was bathed in a flood of golden sunshine. The air was sweet with the breath of roses blooming in the gardens. A thousand flags and pennons and banners fluttered from housetops, floated from tall flag-poles, and waved from open windows. There was music everywhere, and everywhere the tread of moving feet and the gay noise and confusion of a happy crowd.

From the crest of its long sloping hill the new capitol, vast and majestic, looked down on all this life and color. Its massive walls arose like the façade of some proud temple; its pillars of rosy granite reflected the light; its great dome soared into the blue sky. No wonder the people burst into shouts of delight on beholding it!

The dedication ceremonies took place at noon in the presence of an immense throng of citizens and soldiers. Among the orators of the occasion was Temple Houston, a son of

General Sam Houston. The day was one long to be remembered. At night the noble building was illuminated, and the lofty halls and corridors were filled for hours with the best, the bravest, and the fairest of the sons and daughters of Texas.

In the old days when the world still believed in fairies and gnomes and elves and water-sprites, it was thought that each country had its guardian spirit, or genie, who watched over it and protected it from evil. If the poets of those far-away times were now alive, they might picture the Genie of Texas standing, invisible, on the huge dome of the capitol,

New Capitol at Austin (1888).

looking out over her beloved state, and saying, "All is well with my people." They might imagine her describing the scene under her eyes to the guardians of other states in words like these:

"I see around me, widespread and beautiful, the free State of Texas. Below me, clad in flowers and bathed in mellow light, lies Austin. Crowning the hills, on which fifty years ago the Red Man dwelt in his wigwams and hunting-lodges, are stately government buildings, mansions, and churches; and fair in their midst stands the University planned by the Republic in 1839. At the base of Austin's hills the river Colorado, prisoned in its bed by a wonderful granite dam,— the largest in the world,— spreads out into a lake thirty miles long, on whose broad bosom float steamboats and yachts, and whose waters will one day supply the power for busy workshops and factories.

"To southward, beyond prairies threaded by the crystal waters of the rivers San Marcos and Guadalupe, I see San Antonio, that old town filled with memories of heroic deeds. The Alamo, treasured by my people, still stands on the plaza once dyed by the blood of Travis and his men. But how the gallant St. Denis would stare if he could come riding up and look from the brow of his favorite hill into the valley he loved! The village has become a great city. The streets are alive with traffic, handsome houses line the river-banks almost to the old Missions of Concepcion and San José. The United States army post is there as of old, with the stars and stripes proudly waving over its fine buildings.

"To east and southeastward are Goliad and Gonzales, sacred in the pages of Texas history; and the river La Vaca, up which La Salle and his men sailed to build ill-fated Fort St. Louis; and the San Jacinto, washing the reedy edge of the famous battle-ground. There are Houston and Columbia, whose streets in the early days were trod by the fathers of the Republic. There is Nacogdoches; and there is the Old San Antonio Road, which is still a traveled highway; and many a town which played its part in the stirring scenes of past times.

"Northward and westward lies the newer Texas with thriving cities, such as Dallas and Fort Worth, Sherman and Denison; and Waco on the site where half a century ago stood the village of the music-loving Wacoes.

"A wonderful network of railroads binds all these towns and cities together — a network which has been woven as if by magic. In 1852 the *Sidney Sherman*, the first locomotive engine west of the Mississippi River, ran out of Harrisburg on a short stretch of railroad. Now there are nine thousand miles of railroad in the state.

"Every year vast fields of grain lie golden and ripe for the harvest, where a short time ago plover and partridge hid in the prairie grass. Along the coast the rich plantations of sugar cane wave and rustle in the breeze, and the smoke of the sugarhouses at grinding-time is black against the sky.

"In Stephen F. Austin's day there were little patches of cotton about the cabin doors of the settlers. To-day Texas grows one-third of the cotton raised in the world. No fleece so white,

Ashbel Smith.

no stalks so weighted with bursting bolls, no fiber so strong and yet so delicate, as that of the cotton of Texas.

"I see," the Genie might continue, "I see orchards of fruit trees, and vegetable gardens, and rose bowers, making green and glad the face of the country.

"I see at Galveston and Sabine Pass the largest ships now sailing with ease, where in 1863 the *Westfield* and the *Clifton* grounded in mud or on a sand-bar.

"The mysterious and limitless pools and lakes which lie far below the surface of Texas soil have been forced into service.

I see artesian wells spouting their sturdy columns of clear healing water in hundreds of places.

"Herds of cattle swarm about the great ranches of the west; while in the vast unfenced solitudes soft-eyed antelopes, and other wild creatures of the forest, still rove in primeval freedom.

"Last, and best of all, wherever there is a quiet hamlet or a growing town or a busy city, I see a schoolhouse. It may be but a rude cabin, where through the unchinked logs the children may watch the birds building their nests, or it may be a stately building which glorifies the memory of some generous giver, like the Ball and Rosenburg Schools at Galveston; it may be a crowded little place where the boys kick their heels against time-worn benches, or it may be the handsome University of Texas. But big or little, stone building or log cabin, there is always the schoolhouse; and within it the school children, the future men and women of the state. Upon them, even more than upon railroad or cotton crop, depend the prosperity and welfare of the state. I breathe a prayer for all who tread this free and unfettered soil to-day; but chiefly I call down blessings upon the school children of Texas.

"All is well with my people."

So might speak the Genie of Texas from the dome of the capitol.

Texas State Flag.

PRONUNCIATION.

Acequia (Ah sā′ kee ah)
Adaes (Ah dah′ ess)
Aes (Ah′ ess)
Aguayo (Ah gwah′ yo)
Aimable (Ā mah bl)
Alamo (Ah′ lah mo)
Alazan (Ah′ lah zan)
Almonte (Al mon′ tā)
Alvarez (Al′ vah ress)
Ampudia (Am poo′ dee ah)
Anahuac (An′ ah wak)
Andrade (An drah′ dā)
Arredondo (Ar rā don′ do)
Anastase (Ah nas taze′)
Barbier (Bar bee ā)
Beaujeu (Bō zhuh)
Benevidas (Bā nā vee′ das)
Belleisle (Bel eel)
Bexar (Bair)
Bustamente (Boos tā mān′ tā)
Cabet (Cā bā)
Castenado (Kas tā nah′ do)
Champ d'Asile (Chon dazile)
Coahuila (Ko ah wee′ lah)
Colito (Ko lee′ tō)
Cordero (Kor dā ro)
De Pagès (Pa jess)
Desloges (Dā loj)
Duhaut (Du ho)
Elisondo (El ee son′ do)
Espiritu Santo (Ess pee′ ree too)
Filisola (Fee lee sō′ lah)
Garza (Gar′ ssa)
Grand Terre (Gron Tair)
Guadalupe (Gwah dah loop′ ā)
Gutierrez (Goo tee ā′ ress)

Herrera (Ā rā′ rah)
Indios Bravos (In′ dee oss Brah′ voss)
Indios Reducidos (Rā doo see′ doss)
Joli (Zho lie)
José (Ho sā′)
Joutel (Zhoo tel)
La Bahia (Lah Bah ee′ ah)
Martinez (Mar tee′ ness)
Mier (Mee′ ah)
Mina (Mee′ nah)
Moragnet (Mo rah nyā)
Musquis (Moos keess′)
Natchitoches (Nak ee tosh)
Neches (Nā′ chez)
Nika (Nee kah)
Orquisacas (Or kee sah′ kass)
Ory (Ō ree)
Pedro (Pā′ dro)
Perez (Pā ress)
Perote (Pa ro′ ta)
Piedras (Pee ā′ drass)
Plaza (Pla′ zah)
Presidio (Prā see′ dee o)
Refugio (Rā foo′ jee ō)
Saget (Sah jā)
Saltillo (Sal tee′ yo)
San Felipe (Fā lee′ pa)
Santa Fé (Fā)
St. Denis (San De nee)
Toledo (To lā′ do)
Tonti (Ton tee)
Ugartechea (Oo gar ta chā′ ah)
Urrea (Oo rā′ ah)
Zacetacas (Zah kā tah′ kas)
Zavala (Zah vah′ lah)

INDEX.

A Bold Rider, 14.
A Buffalo Hunt, 154.
A Cloud in the Sky, 148.
A Fatal Venture, 29.
A Hurried Ride, 40.
A Treacherous Shot, 46.
A Voice in the Wilderness, 48.
Acequias, 22.
Across the Border, 136.
Adaes, Mission of, 18, 29.
Aes, Mission of, 21, 22, 29.
Agricultural and Mechanical College, 170.
Aguayo, Marquis de, 21, 23.
Aimable, The, 2, 4.
Alamo, The, 18, 27, 71, 81, 82, 103, 176.
Almonte, Colonel, 86, 101, 103, 136.
Along the Old San Antonio Road, 14, 25, 27, 30, 176.
Alvarez, Señora, 95.
Ampudia, General, 128, 138.
An Unexpected Meeting, 56.
Anahuac, Fort, 38, 61.
Anastase, Father, 7.
Andrade, General, 110.
Annexation, 113, 135.
Apaches, The, 19, 24, 30, 142.
Archer, Branch T., 59, 74.
Archives, War of the, 124.
Arredondo, General, 39.

Arroyo Hondo, 36.
Artesian Wells, 178.
Asylums, 141, 172.
Aury, Luis d', 42.
Austin City, 122, 126, 132, 135, 141, 148, 150, 152, 174.
Austin, Moses, 50.
Austin, Stephen F., Character and Appearance, 51.
—— Contract with Martinez, 52.
—— Arrival with Colonists, 52.
—— Journey to Mexico, 53.
—— Return from Mexico, 55.
—— Imprisonment in Mexico, 60.
—— Release from Prison, 62.
—— In Command of Volunteers, 66.
—— Commissioner to United States, 69.
—— Secretary of State, 113.
—— Death and Burial, 113.
Austin's Colonists, 52.

Banks, General, 165.
Barbier, Sieur, 6, 7.
Barry, "Buck," 148.
Bastrop, Baron de, 50, 55.
Battle of the Alamo, 82.
—— of Colita, 91.
—— of Concepcion, 67.
—— of Galveston, 160.
—— of Mier, 128.

INDEX.

Battle of Palo Alto, 137, 165.
—— of Resaca de la Palma, 137.
—— of Rosillo, 38.
—— of Sabine Pass, 164.
—— of Three Trees, 43.
—— of Velasco, 54.
Bay of Bernard, 3, 11, 12.
—— of Matagorda, 3, 156.
Baylor, John R., 155.
Bean, Ellis P., 31, 32, 33.
Beaujeu, 3, 4.
Bell, Hansboro P., 140.
Belle, The, 2, 6.
Belleisle, 11, 12.
Benevidas, Placido, 81.
Bexar, Duke de, 18.
Bienville, Sieur de, 12.
Blackburn, Ephraim, 35.
Blanco, El, 32.
Blockade-running, 159.
Blue, The, and the Gray, 167, 168.
Blue Wing, 144.
Bolivar Point, 46, 48, 53.
Bonham, James, 81, 83, 87.
Bowie, James, 66, 79, 83, 86.
Bowie, Rezin, 43, 80.
Bradburn, Juan Davis, 58.
Brazoria, 55, 85.
Brazos River, 52, 74, 87.
Brown, Captain Jerry, 107, 118.
Brownsville, 137, 165.
Brutus, The, 112, 116, 118, 119.
Buffalo Bayou, 91, 97, 98, 99, 111, 115.
Burleson, Edward, 65, 69, 73, 124, 138.
Burnet, David G., 59, 87, 98, 105, 107, 108, 112, 120.
Burton, Isaac, 112.
Bustamente, 57, 61.
By the Brazos, 74.

Cabet, Etienne, 148.
Calder, Robert, 67, 106.
Caldwell, Matthew, 122, 126.
Canary Islands, 23.
Cannon at Concepcion, 67.
—— at Gonzales, 62.
—— at San Jacinto, 99, 100.
Capital, The, at Austin, 120, 138.
—— at Columbia, 112.
—— at Houston, 115, 126.
—— at San Antonio, 50, 56.
—— at Saltillo, 56, 60.
—— at Washington, 130.
Capitol, Dedication of, 174.
Carankawaes, 5, 10, 42, 43, 77, 142.
Cart War, 141.
Cash, Mrs., 95.
Castenado, Captain, 63.
Castle of Perote, 127, 129, 139.
Castro, Henry, 132.
Cenis, 5, 6, 10, 142.
Champ d'Asile, 44.
Chrisman, Lieutenant, 148.
Clark, Edward, 152.
Clère, Le, 115.
Coahuila, 9, 59.
Coke, Richard, 169.
Colita, Battle of, 92.
Collingsworth, George A., 64.
Colonists, 23, 24, 52, 53, 55.
Colorado River, 52, 122, 176.
Columbia, 111, 112, 113, 176.
Comanches, 9, 19, 24, 30, 121, 140, 142, 147.
Concepcion, Battle of, 67.
—— Mission of, 20, 67, 127.
Confederate States, The, 151, 166.
Congress, The Texan, 105, 113, 115, 122, 126, 132.
Considerant, Victor, 150.
Cordero, Antonio, 55, 59.

INDEX.

Corpus Christi, 137.
Cortina, 151.
Cos, Martin Perfecto de, 61, 66, 72.
Cotton, Captain, 147.
Cotton, Texas, 177.
Council-house Fight, 121.
Coushattis, 45, 142.
Cowl and Carbine, 16.
Crocker, Captain, 165.
Crockett, David, 83, 86, 145.
Culberson, Charles A., 169.
Cushing, E. H., 159.

Davis, E. J., 168.
Davis Guards, 163.
Davis, Jefferson, 138.
Dawson, Nicholas, 127.
Declaration of Independence, 78, 87.
Dedication of Capitol, 174.
De Leon, Alonzo, 9, 10, 15, 77.
De Nava, General, 31, 32.
De Pagès, 29.
Desauque, Captain, 91.
Desloges, 4.
Dickinson, Lieutenant, 83.
—— Mrs., 87, 89.
Dimitt, Captain, 78, 79.
Dimmitt's Point, 4.
Donna Maria, 15.
Dorn, Earl Van, General, 156.
Dowling, Dick, 163.
Duggan, Ensign, 156.
Duhaut, 7.
Dying Races, 142.

Eberle, Mrs., 126.
Education, 123, 141, 169, 178.
Edwards, Hayden, 55.
Elisondo, General Y, 39.
Espiritu Santo, Mission of, 18, 77.
Evans, T. C., 86.

Fannin, James W., 67, 76, 81, 85, 89, 91, 96.
Farias, Gomez, 60.
Fight, The Grass, 68.
Filisola, General, 97, 108.
First Bloodshed, 4.
—— Marriage, 6.
Fisher, William S., 128.
Flag, The Texas, 123.
Ford, John S., 140, 148.
Fort Defiance, 87, 89.
—— Griffin, 163.
—— St. Louis, 1, 5, 10, 13.
Fosset, Captain, 147.
France, 1, 11, 12, 21, 25, 35, 44, 135, 148.
Franciscans, 16, 17, 18, 20, 28.
Franklin, B. C., 166.
Fredonian War, 56.
From the Dome of the Capitol, 174.
Frontenac, Count de, 1, 2.

Galveston, Battle of, 160.
—— City of, 156, 160, 166.
—— Island of, 41, 44, 46, 98, 105, 118, 120, 156, 167.
Garay, Colonel, 95.
Garza, Governor de la, 55.
Genie of Texas, The, 175.
Gil V Barbo, Captain, 30.
Gillentine, Captain, 147.
Godoy, Manuel de, 33.
Goliad, 18, 38, 45, 48, 77, 79, 89, 90, 103, 108.
Gonzales, 62, 85, 97.
Grand Terre, 41, 47.
Granger, General, 166, 167.
Grant, Doctor, 78, 81.
Green, Thomas J., 130.
Greer County, 172.
Griffin, General, 168.

INDEX.

Guadalupe River, 63.
Gutierrez, Bernardo, 37, 39, 40.

Hall, Captain Lee, 148.
Hamilton, A. J., 167.
Harriet Lane, The, 161.
Harrisburg, 97, 98, 105.
Hawkins, Commodore, 107.
Hays, John Coffin, 138, 146.
Henderson, J. P., 135, 137, 140.
Herrera, General, 35, 36, 39.
Hogg, James S., 169.
Home Again, 163.
Houston, City of, 115, 122, 149, 176.
Houston, Sam, Delegate to Convention, 59.
—— With the Army at La Espada, 66.
—— Biography, 74.
—— Commander-in-Chief, 74, 87.
—— Resignation, 80.
—— Retreat, 96.
—— At San Jacinto, 100.
—— Interview with Santa Anna, 103.
—— President of Republic, 112, 124.
—— At Houston, 115.
—— United States Senator, 136.
—— Governor of Texas, 150.
—— Death, 153.
How the Good News was Brought, 105.
Hubbard, Richard B., 169.

Icaria, 148.
In Church and Fortress, 82.
In the Name of France, 1.
—— of Spain, 9.
—— of Oblivion, 12.
Inauguration, Houston's, 112.
Independence, Declaration of, 78, 87.
Indians, Texas, Adaes, 30.
—— Apaches, 19, 24, 30, 142.

Indians, Carankawaes, 5, 10, 42, 43, 77, 142.
—— Cenis, 5, 6, 10, 142.
—— Comanches, 9, 19, 24, 30, 31, 121, 142, 147.
—— Coushattis, 45, 142.
—— Kiowas, 142.
—— Lipans, 11, 140, 142.
—— Nassonites, 5, 142.
—— Naugodoches, 29.
—— Orquisacas, 142.
—— Tehas, 10, 30, 142.
—— Wacoes, 142, 176.
Indios Bravos, 23, 24, 25.
—— Reducidos, 24.
Inscriptions on Alamo Monument, 173.
Institute, Sam Houston Normal, 170.
Ireland, John, 159.
Iron Jacket, 140.
Ironclad oath, 158.

Jetties, The, 172.
Johnson, Frank W., 71, 72, 79, 81.
Johnston, Albert Sidney, 120, 138, 166, 168.
Joli, The, 2.
Jones, Anson, 134, 136.
—— Randall, 40, 54.
Joutel, 7, 8.

Karnes, Henry, 72, 102.
Kemper, Captain, 38, 39.
King, Captain, 89.

La Bahia, 18, 38, 45, 48.
La Espada, Mission of, 23, 66, 68.
La Harpe, Bernard de, 12, 21.
La Salle, Robert, Cavalier de, 1, 9, 12, 49, 143, 176.
La Vaca, 4, 176.
Lafitte, Jean, 40, 44, 46, 157.

INDEX.

Lallemand, General, 44.
Lamar, Mirabeau B., 120, 123, 139.
Las Almagras, 20, 25.
Lea, Edward, 162.
Lee, Robert E., 151, 165.
Les Vaches, 4, 143.
Liberty, The, 117.
Lincoln, Abraham, 151.
Liotot, 7.
Lively, The, 117.
Lockhart, Matilda, 121.
Long, David, 40, 46.
—— General James, 40, 46, 49, 77.
—— Mrs., 40, 46, 48, 53.
Lubbock, F. R., 157.

Magee, Augustus W., 27, 28, 49.
Magruder, John B., 160.
Martinez, Governor, 50, 53.
Massacre at Goliad, 95, 103.
—— at San Saba, 20, 25.
Matagorda Bay, 3, 156.
Matamoras, 78, 137.
McCulloch, Benjamin, 138, 155, 166.
McLeod, General Hugh, 123, 139, 166.
Messengers of Distress, 77.
Mexico, 9, 24, 27, 42, 53, 55, 61, 74, 82, 111, 120, 124, 128, 132, 144.
Mier, Battle of, 128.
Milam, Benjamin, 64, 70, 72.
Military Rule, 167.
Mina Xavier, 42.
Mission of Adaes, 18, 21, 29.
—— of Aes, 18, 21, 22, 29.
—— of Concepcion, 20, 67, 68, 127.
—— of Espada, 23, 60, 68.
—— of Nacogdoches, 18, 29, 48.
—— of Nuestra Señora del Pilar, 22.
—— of Orquisacas, 10, 22, 25.
—— of Refugio, 91.

Mission of San Francisco, 9.
—— of San José, 18, 23, 28, 176.
—— of San Saba, 20, 25.
Missionaries, 17.
Missions, Building of, 17.
Mississippi River, The, 1, 11, 12, 36, 159.
Moderators, 134.
Monclova, 9, 15, 23.
Monterey, Siege of, 138.
Moragnet, 7.
Mother Ditch, The, 22.
Murrah, Pendleton, 167.
Musquiz, 32.
Mustangs, 30, 34.

Nacogdoches, 18, 29, 32, 35, 38, 46, 48, 56, 58, 176.
Nassonites, 5, 142.
Natchitoches, 12, 20, 22, 27, 35, 39, 40, 46.
Navy, The Texas, 117, 120.
Neches River, 7, 9.
Neill, Colonel, 71, 80.
Neptune, The, 160.
Neutral Ground, The, 35, 39, 55, 134.
Nika, 7.
Nolan, Philip, 31, 49.
Norris, Captain J. H., 147.

Odlum, Captain, 163.
Old San Antonio Road, The, 14, 25, 27, 30, 176.
On Buffalo Bayou, 111.
Only Son, The, 53.
Orders and Disorder, 56.
Orquisacas, Mission of, 18, 22, 25.
Ory, 4.
Out of a Mist, 65.
Owasco, The, 161.

INDEX.

Palm Sunday, 91.
Palo Alto, Battle of, 137, 165.
Parker, Cynthia Ann, 150.
Pass, Sabine, 163.
Pease, E. M., 140, 141, 168.
Perez, Colonel, 46.
Perote, Castle of, 127, 129.
Perry, Colonel, 42.
Philippines, The New, 16, 22.
Piedras, Colonel, 58.
Plaza de las Islas, 23, 69.
Plazas, 21, 23, 27, 33, 69.
Pocket, The, 118.
Portilla, Colonel, 101.
Prairie View Normal School, 170.
Presidios, 10, 14, 16, 17.
Pride, The, 41, 47, 157.

Railroad Commission, 172.
Railroads, Texas, 159, 177.
Reconstruction Time, 169.
Red House, The, 40, 46.
Red Rovers, The, 76.
Refugio, 80, 90, 91.
Regulators, 134.
Renshaw, Commodore, 161.
Resaca de la Palma, Battle of, 137.
Revenge, The, 53.
Ripley, Harry, 92, 96.
—— Eleazer Wheelock, 92.
Roberts, O. M., 169.
Rose, Moses, 85.
Rosillo, Battle of, 38.
Ross, Lawrence Sullivan, 150, 169.
—— S. P., 140.
Runnels, Hardin R., 140.
Rusk, Thomas J., 87, 89, 108, 110, 136.

Sabine Pass, 63.
—— River, 21, 34, 37.

Saget, 7.
Sal Colorado, The, 137.
Salado, Battle of, 126.
—— Hacienda of, 128.
Sam Houston Normal Institute, The, 170.
San Antonio, 14, 18, 21, 23, 39, 45, 50, 56, 82, 83, 155, 176.
San Bernard, Bay of, 3, 12.
San Felipe de Austin, 50, 56, 62, 65, 69, 74, 76.
San Fernando Church, 24.
San Francisco, Mission of, 10.
San José, Mission of, 18, 23, 28, 176.
San Patricio, 55, 81.
San Pedro River, 83.
San Saba Mission, 20, 25.
Sandoval, Colonel, 65, 177.
Santa Anna, 58, 60, 83, 87, 96, 97, 102, 108, 124, 129, 131, 137, 139.
Santa Fé Expedition, 123, 139.
School, Prairie View Normal, 170.
Schools, Texas, 123, 141, 169, 178.
Scott, General Winfield, 139.
Seal, The Texas, 111.
Secession of Texas, 152.
Shackleford, Doctor, 76, 95.
Sherffius, Henry, 159.
Sheridan, General, 167.
Sherman, General Sidney, 100.
—— Lieutenant, Sidney, 162.
Sibley Expedition, 157.
Slave Ships, 43.
Smith, Ashbel, 134, 171.
—— Benjamin Fort, 108.
—— Deaf, 77, 100.
—— Henry, 74, 75, 76, 111.
—— James, 134.
—— Rev. W. T., 64.
Somervell, General Alexander, 127.
Spain, 9, 11, 21, 25, 28, 33, 35.

INDEX.

St. Denis, Juchereau, 14, 20, 25, 49, 176.
St. Francis, The, 2, 3, 9.
St. John the Baptist, Presidio of, 15, 27.
Star of the West, The, 155, 156.
Stephenson, Rev. Henry, 49, 76.
Stockdale, Fletcher S., 167.
Storming of San Antonio, 71.

Taylor, General Zachary, 137.
Teal, Henry, 108.
Tehas, The, 15, 30, 142.
Texas Ranger, The, 143.
The Blue and the Gray, 167, 168.
The Capital, 120.
The Champ d'Asile, 44.
The Disputed Boundary Line, 33.
The Grays, 68.
The *Invincible*, 107, 117, 119.
The *Pride*, 41, 47, 157.
The Priest's House, 69.
"The Republic is no more," 132.
The Telegraph, 159.
The War of the Archives, 134.
Thirty Years, 167.
Three Trees, Battle of, 43.
Throckmorton, James W., 167.
Toledo, General, 39.
Tonti, Chevalier de, 1, 7, 8.
Totten, Captain, 147.
Travis, William B., 58, 66, 81, 83, 85, 87.
Treasure, Lafitte's, 47.
Twiggs, General David, 156.
Twin Sisters, The, 97, 100.

Ugartechea, Colonel, 58, 72.
United States, The, 36, 42, 46, 56, 57, 69, 113, 120, 135, 136, 139, 144, 152, 166.
University, The Texas State, 120, 170, 178.
Ups and Downs, 52.
Urrea, General, 81, 82, 90, 92, 103.

Vasques, Rafael, 125.
Velasco, Battle of, 58.
Villescas, Governor, 15.
Vince's Bridge, 100.
Virginia Point, 107, 161.

Wacoes, 142, 176.
Wainwright, Commodore, 161.
Walker, Samuel H., 131, 139.
War, The Civil, 155, 166.
War Time Arithmetic, 158.
Ward, Colonel William, 75, 90.
Washington on the Brazos, 87, 131.
Wharton, William H., 59, 66.
Wilkinson, General, 31, 35.
Williamson, R. M., 61, 63.
Woll, General, 126, 130.
Woods, George T., 138, 140.
—— Gonzales, 127.
Wright, Captain Tom, 148.
Wyatt, Captain, 76.

Yellowstone, The, 105, 108.

Zacetacas, 17.
Zavala, Lorenzo D., 87.

www.ingramcontent.com/pod-product-compliance
Lightning Source LLC
Chambersburg PA
CBHW071446150426
43191CB00008B/1256